POWER POINTS IN PERSUASION

POWER POINTS IN PERSUASION

MIKE SOMDAL

Fleming H. Revell Company
Old Tappan, New Jersey

Library of Congress Cataloging-in-Publication Data
Somdal, Mike.
  Power Points in Persuasion

  Bibliography: p.
  1. Success in business. 2. Selling—Psychological aspects. 3. Persuasion (Psychology) I. Title.

HF5386.S735 1986   650.1   86-3827
ISBN 0-8007-1481-4

TO my customers,
who have made possible my
fulfilling advertising career,
and without whom this book
would not have been written

PART I
WINNING TAKES PLANNING—SO PLAN TO WIN

Part II
GO FOR THE SALE EARLY AND OFTEN

PART III
A LITTLE MORE EFFORT CAN MEAN A LOT MORE SUCCESS

POWER
POINTS
IN
PERSUASION

Why I Wrote This Book

There are really no "pat answers"—easy answers to life's complex questions. So the logical question is, why the title *P*A*T* Answers: Power Points in Persuasion?*

Good question.

It happened accidentally (many book titles come to life accidentally, I have discovered) during a conversation I was having with my good friend and neighbor Ray Zoref, after I had written most of the book.

"Have you figured out what you're going to call it?" asked Ray.

"I think so," I said. "The publisher and I have tentatively agreed it's going to be *Power Points in Persuasion.*"

Ray looked at me with a blank stare. "What does that mean?" he asked.

I explained that I really had thought about that a lot—and what I've tried to say in the book is that the person who has learned how to successfully persuade someone to his point of view has developed three primary "power points": the ability to say what he wants to say persuasively (the right *phrasing*); positive motivation and an upbeat way of looking at his persuasive attempts (the right *attitude*); and the absolutely essential facility for making his argument at the most effective moment (the right *timing*).

Ray pondered that, then said aloud, "So your book is about persuading people by using the right phrasing, attitude, and timing. Why don't you create a word out of the first initial of those three words—*phrasing, attitude,* and *timing*—and call it *How to Get Your Selling Down P.A.T.*"

From that off-the-cuff but inspired suggestion, the title for this book was eventually created, and is one that describes

13

what you will find in the pages inside. A word about Ray's first suggestion: It is important to note that *P*A*T* Answers* is not just for those in selling (although it will certainly be helpful to professionals who make their living persuading people to their point of view). In a much larger sense, it is a book for everyone who wants to master "phrasing, attitude, and timing," and improve persuasive techniques in the process.

There are many people who helped to make this book a reality and they deserve a few words of gratitude. I am deeply indebted to the staff at Revell for their faith in me and their support of this project from the beginning. To all my close friends, who always knew I "wanted to be an author when I grew up," a warm thank you for your support, interest, and encouragement. To my wife, Linda, daughter, Jennifer, and son, Kirk—thanks, family, for your patience, your love, and especially your indulgence while I struggled, often moodily, through the creative process.

Finally, a word of deep appreciation for my close friend, writing mentor, and inspiration, Dr. Alan Loy McGinnis. A best-selling author himself, Loy has always encouraged me to write and to fulfill my lifelong ambition to be an author. I have done that, encouraged in large part by his example, and for that I will always be grateful.

And now, a special word to you, the reader. I want what I have to say about persuasion to be of help to you. I think it can be, because it is based on what I have done throughout my career in advertising sales: persuading others successfully to my point of view. You can be a successful persuader yourself—if you choose to—and *P*A*T* Answers: Power Points in Persuasion* can be your catalyst for getting started. Good luck in all your persuasive efforts. And I sincerely hope you enjoy the book.

MIKE SOMDAL

PART I

WINNING TAKES PLANNING— SO PLAN TO WIN

ONE

You Can Develop
the Power to Persuade

Persistent people begin their success where others end in failure.

Edward Eggleston

This is a book about power—the kind of personal, persuasive power you can develop and use in critical situations, day after day. Whether you are a teacher, mother or father, manager or salesperson, you are constantly confronted with situations in which you must persuade someone to your point of view.

For many, it is an awesome task. How to persuade, what to say, and when to say it are vital questions for each of us, but questions which may be put aside or ignored because we don't consider ourselves salespeople or identify selling as something we must do. However, our ability to sell ourselves in whatever we do may often mean the difference between success and failure. As my friend Cherry Henricks, partner in her own interior-design firm, told me recently, "We like to think that our business is designing first and selling second, but it isn't. We have to sell ourselves and the services we offer before we can do the job we were trained to do."

Cherry points out very clearly the value of selling in her chosen profession, and that she has to be a successful salesperson before she can be an interior designer. The same holds true for the vocational counselor selling an employer on the value of seeing his applicant, for the manager of a large manufacturing company selling his employees on increasing their productivity, for the volunteer who must enlist the support of other volunteers for a specific charity fund raiser. None of these people started out to be professional persuaders, or salespeople, and may not think of themselves in that way. But the fact is, none of them could exist in their businesses without perfecting the art of persuasion.

The Keys to Unlocking Your Persuasive Power

P*A*T* Answers will show you how to focus on the critical elements of any sales or persuasive situation, and then use just the right combination of phrasing, attitude, and timing to seize the initiative and move toward the proper resolution of the problem. This book will emphasize key steps you can take before, during, and after your sales or persuasion interview to increase your chances for making the sale.

An ancient cliché is that great salesmen are made, not born. That is as true today as it ever was, and it is a major reason I decided to write this book. Over the last eighteen years I have worked in the advertising business, with most of those years spent as sales manager for a large chain of community newspapers in Los Angeles. I have seen many sales successes and many sales failures, both in and out of my company, but the one overriding factor common in all cases was this: Those salespeople who were most successful had timing and phrasing down to a fine art, while those who floundered in failure never knew when to do or say the important things necessary to close a deal.

Good Salespeople Make Things Happen

Most of us expect professional salespeople to be proficient in the art of persuasion—and rightly so. But alas—we are so often frustrated by such a monumental lack of knowledge, enthusiasm, persistence, creativity, and sensitivity from many who call themselves salespeople, that it is a wonder we are ever sold our automobiles, insurance policies, televisions, toasters, and all the other products we buy from them.

It seems as though at times a challenge or the word *no* are insurmountable obstacles for many in selling, when in reality that's when a salesperson should feel the most challenged, the most exhilarated, because his prospect is telling him what is wrong with what he is presenting and what he needs to do to make his offer more attractive. The *nos*, the turndowns, the rejections which come to all salespeople, are just the starting points for those who succeed in selling . . . their jumping-off point to find a way, develop a plan, think of an ingenious reason someone should buy what they are selling. Imagine, for example, the enthusiasm created by this advertising salesman during the following sales presentation taking place in the fifth-floor conference room of a major retail department store—a presentation in danger of going nowhere.

The young newspaper executive was very close to making his first major sale and was caught in a terrible dilemma—what to do during that awful silence as the prospect pondered the offer. He considered saying nothing, but then suddenly remembered that the biggest objection appeared to be additional cost. "You know, Mr. Barkman, I think I can save you some money and really make your advertising investment worthwhile. We have a special six-week advertising contract which will allow you to reduce your rate by ten percent while giving our newspaper enough ads to see if we can produce."

Replying hesitantly, Barkman said, "Well, I don't know. . . ."

The salesman reacted quickly. Sensing that he had begun to turn the tide, but that there was still some lingering doubt, he decided to put everything on the line.

"Mr. Barkman, if my newspaper doesn't increase your sales dramatically during the few weeks of the test, you'll never have to put up with me again. But if it pulls the way I know it will, we'll have a lot to talk about."

"All right," said Barkman. "I've decided to give your paper a try. But if it doesn't bring some results by the end of those six weeks, I'm pulling out."

"You're absolutely right. And it's a fair test. But I'm convinced this is the start of a long and happy relationship." Shaking hands, the two parted company, each convinced that they had gained something in the transaction.

Very early in my sales career, this particular scenario happened almost exactly as I have described it. The postscript on the story is that Barkman's sales did increase dramatically once he started using our paper, and he in turn gave us several years of uninterrupted furniture advertising, week in and week out.

Over the years, I have often thought back to that first important success, especially in times of major sales distress (they
happen to everyone who makes a living persuading people)
to exactly what it was I did to turn the corner with the
prospect.

Obviously, I took a risk at a time when the sale just as easily
could have been lost. And I was so sure of my product that I
laid the whole future of our relationship with Barkman's company on the line if the advertising test I was proposing didn't
work. It was a bold approach—made bolder, perhaps, by my
youthful confidence—but I was able to convince the prospect
at just the right time with both my special advertising offer and
my sincerity, a combination he found too irresistible to turn
down. I had the P*A*T* Answers—the right words, said in
the right way at the right time.

In the hundreds of selling situations I have encountered
every year as National Advertising Manager and now as General Manager for the *Wave* newspapers, the selling signals are
rarely as loud and clear as this example. Most require much
more resourcefulness in discovering the objections and decid-
ing when to pursue the prospect with the inevitable question:
Will you buy what I am selling?

What Would You Do to Persuade Your Prospect?

What would you do in a similar situation? Would you have
either the courage to remain silent, or to be bold, depending
on the situation? Or are you thinking that you could never
manage either approach?

The good news is that you are not alone and that you can
learn the fine art of sales timing—when to say just the right
thing at just the right time, and for the right reasons.

Those who master the art of selling, who know how and when to make something happen, who can "read" the subtle nuances in a selling situation as they are happening and react accordingly, and who have the best interests of their prospects at heart as well as their own, all have one thing in common: the tremendous sense of self-satisfaction that comes from success in persuading others.

That's probably one of the main reasons you've picked up this book: to achieve greater persuasive success than you currently enjoy. And when you achieve that success, you can reap the extra benefits enjoyed by those who master the art of selling in their chosen fields. These include above-average incomes and all the material trappings that come with such success— comfortable homes, well-planned retirements, tremendous self-gratification, and positions of stature in their communities.

Average or Successful—It's Your Choice

However, most people will never achieve this super state of advanced income and status. As Robert Shook points out in his excellent little book *Ten Greatest Salespersons,*

> ... given similar territories, and [the fact that] they sell the same product ... it's general knowledge that 20 percent of all salespeople make 80 percent of the sales. Immediately, these disproportionate figures inform us that a salesperson in the top 20 percent sells at a rate sixteen times higher than the rate of salesmen in the lower 80 percent.[1]

Master the principles in this book and you can go from the lower 80 percent to the upper 20 percent. It's possible, and it can happen to you if you remain sensitive to all those with whom you come in contact, and responsive as much as it is possible to their needs.

Phrasing—Finding the Right Word at the Right Time

Sometimes we are afforded a rare opportunity to touch someone's life with a kind word of assurance or vote of confidence uttered at just the right time. I was given that opportunity during a recent sales trip to the East Coast. I was tired and had just entered my fifth cab of the day when I saw a sign that read "God Bless This Car" affixed to the glove compartment. That sign became the breakthrough for an animated conversation during the short ride to the train station.

"I've given up drinking now," the cabdriver said suddenly. "I was on a twenty-three-year honeymoon, and when my wife died two years ago, I drank anything and everything I could get my hands on."

He told me about his struggles to bring up his children, one of whom was constantly in trouble with the police. "It's slowly changing," he sighed, weariness in his voice. "I'm remarried, and my wife is good with the kids. The boy's got a job, finally, yet I still can't seem to reach him. . . ." His words trailed off as the station came into view.

Touched by his openness, I felt compelled to stop and give some encouragement, even though I was close to missing my train. "Things are looking up," I said quietly. "You've beaten your drinking problem, are remarried, and now your boy's working. God's really smiling on you, and He'll help you see the bright side."

I had started to get out of the cab when he turned and said, "You know, you're right. I have a lot to be thankful for, but I hardly ever think about the positive side of things." Then, after a brief pause, he said, "Thanks. You really helped me." He drove off and I boarded my train, moved at how the right words at the right time seemed to persuade him of his worth and his value to his family.

Can You Walk a Mile in Their Shoes?

For some reason, I was in the right place at the right time and said the right thing to my cabdriver friend. We were very tuned in to each other, and there was some high energy in that conversation, symbolized by a genuine desire on the part of the cabdriver to learn and a sincere dsesire on my part to help. The timing was right for me to tell him exactly what I thought would help him at that moment.

Selling is a lot like that. It can be a wonderful experience when you feel genuine concern and interest in the person you are trying to persuade or to sell your point of view. Whether you are trying to form a committee for a neighborhood organization, reach a child who has become distant and uncommunicative, or trying to sell people your product or service, you will have more long-range success and feel better about it if you can walk a mile in their shoes. In your selling and persuasive efforts, be open, sensitive, and caring to everyone.

In other words, make your prospect's needs just as important as your needs. They are, you know. In fact, they are *more* important, because if they are not met, your previously successful persuasive presentation can unravel more quickly than you thought possible. So take the time to know your prospect, and know *about* your prospect—leisure time, activities, vacation plans, family, friends. Be genuine, be available, and be a friend, and you'll be amazed at how much more you will get out of your relationship with that person.

A Caring Attitude Means Lasting Relationships

In the process of showing care and concern toward your prospect, an astonishing thing could happen: You might make a sale. Frank Bettger, a phenomenally successful insurance salesman, wrote a book on selling that is still widely read years after his death. In this best-seller, *How I Raised Myself From Failure to Success in Selling*, he tells how his own sensitivity and caring about another man's needs helped him discover one of the most resounding truths in sales today: "Find Out What People Want, and Help Them Get It."

Bettger realized a big commission from the sale he describes in the book, and recounts the day he realized his client was concerned with more than just a single life insurance policy.

Suddenly it occurred to me that he had *another* job to take care of, planning the future of his business. He had gone into great detail with me about how he came to America from Ireland as a lad of seventeen, took a job in a small grocery store, finally started his own business and gradually built one of the finest wholesale grocery businesses in the East. Naturally he had a sentimental feeling for that business. It was his life work. Surely he wanted it to continue long after he passed away. Within thirty days after I returned from the Boston convention, I helped John Scott work out a plan to take his sons and eight other employees into the business with him. . . . The insurance I placed on the lives of all those key men in the business, including additional amounts on Mr. Scott, resulted in a sale paying me more money in one day than I had ever earned previously in an entire year of selling.[2]

Frank Bettger had made something happen by listening
carefully and being sensitive to what his prospect wanted, and
then constructing a plan that would enable him to get it. By
selling him just what he needed, nothing more and nothing
less, he created trust and confidence in the relationship.

Timing—Essential Ingredient for Success

In my own surveys of the available sales literature, I have
found precious little written about the salesman's inability to
take advantage of timing in his chosen profession. Small wonder, then, that a small percentage of salespeople have the greatest share of sales success, with the great majority of salespeople
never able to rise above an average or mediocre level in their
careers.

Timing. What an enigma. Those who invested in gold when
it was thirty-two dollars an ounce had excellent timing, while
those who wanted to cash in on seemingly guaranteed profits
by investing in gold after it had soared to over eight hundred
dollars per ounce had terrible timing. Most people want to say
the right thing at the right time, but can't quite comprehend
how to do it. It sounds so simple, but oh, how most of us wres-
tle with trying to avoid inserting foot in mouth.

We all have embarrassing moments, including those people
who make their living persuading others. Early in my advertising career, before I joined the newspaper, I was with an advertising agency in Los Angeles and was being groomed to take
over a particular account. The ad manager I was to meet was
known to be difficult to deal with, and I had only known of
him from seeing him around the agency several times before.
Heavyset, bald, and famous for exploding in anger at the

slightest provocation, he was a formidable client, and I was really dreading my meeting with him.

I was unnerved when my boss and I were ushered into the office of this tough individual, only to see him with a brand-new, full head of hair! Somehow I managed to take my eyes off of this resplendent new hairpiece and focus on the business at hand. After our brief meeting, which was really arranged so that I could meet him, I felt it was time to go and uttered these immortal words: "Thanks for your time. We'll get out of your hair now." At that moment, I broke out in a cold sweat and my eyes, as if magnetized, shot up to the new piece of fuzz residing atop my client's head. In my mind, the next few seconds took hours to pass, punctuated only by my pounding heart and my prayer to become invisible on the spot.

I survived. The client either didn't hear or didn't acknowledge the obvious faux pas of a young executive who thought he was certain to die of hoof-and-mouth disease. During the following months, I actually got along very well with this man whom I had been dreading, and I learned a valuable lesson at the same time. No matter how good we are or how good we *think* we are, we are all capable of making very human mistakes at the worst possible moments. If we can learn from our mistakes and laugh at them—and I have often laughed at that poor choice of words—then we will become better at everything we do, including the job of relating to other people throughout our lives. What I try to emphasize to all of my salespeople is this:

Don't dwell on your mistakes—learn from them.

Roadblocks to Effective Selling

Up to now you might be thinking, *It's one thing to say you should have the correct phrasing, attitude, and timing, and an-*

other thing to actually know how and when to use each of
these techniques in specific selling situations.

It isn't really that difficult after all, especially once you've
come to grips with your own problems or inadequacies in selling and have a genuine desire to change and become better in
the art of persuasion. For it's a fact that when most failures
ask, "Why is life doing this terrible thing to me?" the answer—at least for most failed salespeople—lies in the face in
the mirror.

But it doesn't have to be that way. If we can learn to care for
and respect the people we are selling, learn to work through
our failures and never give up, and above all, approach all selling situations intelligently and enthusiastically, we will be on
our way to fashioning a blueprint for success that will be
greater than anything we have ever achieved in our selling or
persuasive efforts.

You Can Turn Your Weaknesses Into Strengths

Success in selling is waiting for you if you'll begin to analyze
how to influence the turning points in your presentations, and
learn to perfect the techniques presented here. You can begin
this process today, by understanding the things that are keeping you from selling, confronting them, and then learning to
overcome them. Begin with a self-analysis of what you feel are
your biggest problems in selling or persuasion. Write them
down, be challenged by them, and meet them head-on. Then,
write down a list of what you want to accomplish in your selling efforts, and when. At the end of that list, write the word
SUCCESS, for that is what you will have once you learn to
face up to your selling problems, accept the responsibility for
remedying them, and then work hard, using the techniques

suggested here to become the success you always knew you would become.

What we are talking about is drive, desire, and dedication. The ability to persuade can be tough to master—and the business of sales is competitive. Everyone knows that. So what is it that sets you apart from everyone else? As we've said before, it is an inner power—a confidence that comes from knowing you developed just the right combination of words and uttered them at just the right time. Bolstering your confidence is the knowledge that you've done your homework—that you know everything about your product and your prospect, so that you can respond automatically, when the timing is right, with an answer that will seem spontaneous but that was in reality the product of hours of careful research. And finally, you'll know you're ready when you can hardly wait to make the presentation because you know, deep down inside, that you're going to succeed. You have a winning attitude, and it's going to affect everything from how you announce yourself to the receptionist to how you present your final, convincing arguments.

Incredible? Fantastic? How could you pull it off, you ask? Simply by learning how to do it because you want it badly enough. Because you want to have more success in sales than you've ever had before, by applying yourself, facing your weaknesses, and discovering what a tremendous resource you have in yourself if you will but use and develop the gifts God has already given you.

This book is a start, but only a start. In its pages, you will find a plan for success based on principles that have worked for me. But in the end, when it is time to really persuade or to sell, that will be up to you. You will be the one putting these principles to work either out in the marketplace or in your other business and personal relationships. Can you do it? Will it work? Can you make convincing arguments? Can you sell more than you did before? Can you persuade someone to do something you never thought possible?

That, after all, is the biggest unanswered question of them all, and half the fun and challenge of developing the power to persuade.

TWO

Surround Yourself
With Success

We do not know, in most cases, how far social failure and success are due to heredity, and how far to environment. But environment is the easier of the two to improve.

J.B.S. Haldane

Somebody said it couldn't be done, but he with a chuckle replied that "maybe it couldn't," but he would be one who wouldn't say so till he'd tried.

Edgar A. Guest

The professional outlook for Los Angeles Laker basketball star Mitch Kupchak was not bright. He had suffered three hor-

31

rendous injuries to his leg and knee after one fall during a game and would be out for the rest of the season. Most fans in Los Angeles who read the sports pages and listened to the sports shows knew that. They also knew that the injury had happened to a man who had suffered two other serious injuries. Despite that he still played with the all-out abandon and selfless style of team play that had become his trademark in college and during his few up-and-down, injury-plagued seasons in the National Basketball Association.

What most people did not know was that Kupchak's leg was broken so severely, no one held any hope for him ever playing basketball again. As one newspaper account put it two years later:

> The consensus was it was the worst injury ever for an NBA player. A dedicated pro football lineman, whose position doesn't require much running, might come back from such a hurt, but certainly not a running back or a basketball player.[1]

No one held hope, that is, except Kupchak himself. When most of those around him were just hoping he would walk normally again, Mitch Kupchak was preparing for the day when he would come back to play basketball for the Lakers.

Two operations and several months later, Kupchak exercised and exercised, often alone, hour after hour, day after day, to restore the strength in his damaged leg. Yes, he heard the reports of the experts, the predictions he would never play again. He became depressed, as anyone else in his situation would. But it didn't last very long. He didn't let it. Somehow he knew he would come back. He was absolutely determined, and he refused to listen to others, instead preferring to surround himself with his own goal of successful rehabilitation, and with the little signs he wrote and placed all over his apartment. "Yes I can," they said, simple eloquence packaged in a powerful phrase. Notes of encouragement—of success—written *from* Mitch Kupchak *to* Mitch Kupchak.

And slowly the strength returned to his leg. By inches. By degrees. But it returned against all odds, against the pronouncements and predictions of others. Kupchak's leg grew stronger and stronger until, one day in the 1984 season, he stepped back onto a basketball court in a Los Angeles Laker uniform to a thundering ovation from the fans he had always believed would see him play again. That he wore a special leg-length brace and had a backup role on his team didn't bother Kupchak on that day. What mattered was that he had succeeded, beyond all hope or reason. And his road back culminated in the pinnacle of success for a basketball player, the 1984-85 Lakers' victory over the Boston Celtics in the NBA championship series, a series in which Kupchak made invaluable contributions to his team's success.

Privately, Kupchak knew why he had succeeded—partly because he had refused to be limited by the perceptions of other people of what he could do. " 'What's a miracle?' Kupchak asks. 'There are no limitations. The only limits placed on you are the ones put on you by someone else.' "[2] But mostly he succeeded because he—Mitch Kupchak—had wanted to come back and play this most physically demanding of all games so badly that he had set only one goal for himself: the successful rehabilitation of his leg, which would allow him to play basketball and make a meaningful contribution again. Nothing less would do.

As Mitch Kupchak knew and as W. Clement Stone, the highly successful insurance salesman and entrepreneur, has observed, "Success is achieved by those who try. When there is nothing to lose by trying and a great deal to gain if successful, by all means try."[3] There is a lesson here for those who don't want to settle for less:

Don't ever place limits on the pursuit of your goals.

Are You Totally Committed to Success?

Can you be as committed to success in your sales or persuasive efforts as Mitch Kupchak was to the rehabilitation of his leg? Are you committed to succeed against all odds? And are you willing to put in the work and effort required to achieve success? Or are you willing to settle for less, to let others impose limits on you, to define for you just how far you can go in your chosen endeavors? I call this the "challenge of commitment," and it is the very first question you must answer in your quest for success. Simply putting forth a halfhearted effort won't do, as this story illustrates:

> In my office I have a little old sign that I picked up years ago that has a picture of a tramp on it. The tramp is saying, "I'd give a thousand dollars to be one of them millionaires." Now that message is worth just a smile or two until you get down and explore the hidden truth behind it. Hundreds of thousands of salesmen are in the same boat with that tramp. They'd give a thousand dollars' worth of effort and wish for a million dollars in results. They've never made an all-out effort to really turn on the heat and sell. They're so used to just getting by that they've never really gotten a picture of what it means to go first class.[4]

Have you got a million-dollar destination with a thousand-dollar road map? Think over your commitment to success carefully, and take it very seriously, for in the process you'll find out just how prepared you are to succeed.

Donald J. Moine put it very succinctly in an article he wrote for *Psychology Today* on selling. Said Mr. Moine:

> Sales, perhaps more than any other profession, is a psychological laboratory for testing human intelligence, persistence, persuasiveness and resilience: the ability to deal with rejection on a daily basis. As Pat Knowles, one of the top oil and gas tax-shelter sales experts in the nation, told me, "Every day, my prospects and customers beat me and scratch me and kick me and claw me, but I persist, and I help them solve their tax problems. And I walk away with big commissions."[5]

That "nothing succeeds like success" seems obvious enough, but what may not seem as obvious is how to get there.

The Environment of Success

What is apparent to students of human behavior, however, is that success begets success, and positive results are bred from a positive environment—that is, your family, friends, and job situations. So take stock for a minute, and see what kind of environments—positive or negative—you are in from day to day. It could play a big part in your sales success and your attitude toward your job and task at hand.

My wife, Linda, is a beautiful, supportive person who is respected as thoughtful, upbeat, and one who naturally thinks the best of everyone and everything around her. Yet I can recall a brief period when our children were small that she had very little to say and appeared moody and depressed. During this time, she would frequently bring up Rachel, a woman Linda had met when we first moved into the neighborhood.

It seemed that whatever my wife did was discounted by Rachel. She should listen to Rachel and "her way of doing things," which was always superior to my wife's way in Rachel's eyes. I could see that Rachel was not only a perpetual "Negative Nellie," she was actually bringing my wife down to her level, which included berating all of Linda's accomplishments during the latter stages of their relationship.

This friendship, fragile at best, finally disintegrated. There was no dramatic separation from Rachel, but as the two "friends" gradually drifted apart, I saw the return of my happy, upbeat wife as she developed stronger, lasting friendships with people as kind and supportive as she is. Rachel had tried to mold her into a personality shape that didn't fit her character in any way. It was inevitable that this friendship would end, even though no one officially ended it. They just didn't fit each other's image of what a friend was like, and so each moved on to others who did.

Obviously, you can't change or be expected to change the negative opinions of those around you. But you can remain strong in your beliefs and know when you are being dragged down to someone else's level. And remember this important rule:

Associate with those who will lift you up and validate your accomplishments.

Be a 100 Percent Believer in What You Are Selling

In business, it can be just as critical that you recognize those among your associates who can not only separate you from your goal but who can—and very well might—bring you down to their level. And it can happen to anyone, and it did to me when I first began to work at the *Wave.*

I worked in a small branch office several miles away from the main office and was eager and enthusiastic the first day on the new job. Anxious to make a good impression—and new friends—I accepted an invitation to have coffee with a couple of salesmen who had been at the *Wave* for several years. During that fifteen-minute period, I was both shocked and amazed at how down on the company these two veteran employees seemed to be. To hear them tell it, there were problems in every department and it was a wonder the paper ever got out or even existed in the first place.

At first, my mind shot back to the last days I had spent at my former job at the advertising agency. Many of them were filled with whispered portents of doom about my career. "He's going to a *weekly* newspaper." "As National Advertising Manager." "What national advertiser wants to buy ads in a weekly newspaper?" Although I had friends there who supported me, there were others who were quite sure I would fail—the "Negative Nellies" of our office. I was so sure of the newspaper and my chance to succeed that I had just put those comments out of my mind—until now, when they all came flooding back to me from the mouths of my new associates, men who had been at the *Wave* for years and should be in a position to know. Was it true? Had I made a terrible mistake?

And then I made a decision. I put away the doubts and indecisiveness and turned to my two new colleagues with feelings of anger and loyalty to my new company. "I'm really sorry you feel that way," I said. "But as far as I'm concerned, the problems you've outlined don't exist, and I have no reason to think they do. I've got a job to do, and I'm going to believe the best about the company that has hired me to do it until I find out otherwise." With that, I excused myself from the coffee break, and had very little to do with those two men during my first few weeks at the *Wave*.

Why did I avoid them? Because I decided that while what

they were telling me might be true, it had a far better chance *not* to be true. I didn't need their negative input while I was in the early stages of trying to establish myself. And who was I working for, anyway—the two salesmen or the man who had hired me?

With the answer to that question very clear, I didn't ignore the issues that were raised in that coffee break, but I made a point of finding the answers naturally, as I grew in the job and the company.

Happily, and just as I had thought, the questions those men had raised were either totally untrue or gross exaggerations of common problems shared by all newspapers. Well, during the *next* coffee break I went to with those two men, I took great pains to point out what I had learned, and finished the conversation with a suggestion that they check their facts before they started spreading rumors to newly hired people.

Watch How Successful Salespeople Work

Whether or not those around you are negative, it is imperative that you discover the bright side of every selling situation. For many sales experiences will certainly be negative, given the nature of selling. When you are feeling down, and you've managed to avoid those negative individuals around you, what is it that's going to "pick you up" and get you started on the right track again?

A good part of that answer will come from the homework you've already done in your company or organization. What is the company like? What are its strong points, the assets upon which to build a successful sales argument? When I was beset by doubts early in my *Wave* career from what seemed like a mountain of rejections, I had only to watch and learn from the best salesperson in the company, Larry Hews, who was also my boss and mentor. I watched closely how he did what he did, and although his style was and is very different from mine, I learned much from him about salesmanship in general and newspaper advertising in particular.

Who are the great salespeople in your company you admire? Or, if you're not in selling but are reading this book to pick up some pointers on the art of persuasion, you can still look to the great persuaders among your close friends or acquaintances. Get to know these people better. Invite them out to lunch or coffee and share with them your eagerness to learn. I have found that people who are successful in their selling efforts are usually confident, likable people who will probably be flattered and happy to pass on some tricks of the trade you may not have thought of before. In other words:

Get to know the successes in your business—
and learn from them.

Learn to Build on Your Successes

Anyone who has achieved success in selling has faced many of the same problems you face: rejection, doubts, depression. And yet, those we label "successes" somehow come on to win, often persisting in the face of the toughest adversity possible. Equally impressive, most of these people have somehow learned how to build on their successes and to repeat them time after time.

Seeking out and finding examples of great sales successes, coupled with a positive mental outlook, can provide a needed boost at a critical time during the sales process. During those lonely moments when nothing seems to go right, and you doubt you could persuade anyone to do anything, your mind just might call up an example of someone who has succeeded in a similar situation and that can give you the extra inspiration and determination to succeed yourself.

One of the greatest successes in sports history—some say *the* greatest success—is a man who coached UCLA to ten national college basketball championships during his tenure there. And the fact that John Wooden did this in little more than a decade after he had won his first championship bears out the fact that he certainly knew how to build on his past successes.

But Wooden didn't just build winning basketball teams. He built character, principles, and values in the young men who played for him. And one very special thing he did for them was to show them how he thought success could be achieved. Not through shortcuts. Not by luck, but through solid, hard work. Over his years as coach, and after hundreds of hours, Wooden came up with his unique "Pyramid of Success." At the beginning of every basketball season, and at the start of every basketball camp, he made it a point to discuss the pyramid and give everyone a copy of it. At its base is industriousness, friendship, loyalty, cooperation, and enthusiasm. At the pinnacle, competitive greatness, with other solid life values and attitudes making up the rest of the pyramid. Summing up, he says, "Success is peace of mind, which is a direct result of self-satisfaction in knowing you did your best to become the best that you are capable of becoming."[6]

It's easy to see why John Wooden was such a great success as a coach, and continues to command tremendous respect throughout the world. And it is easy to see why so many great basketball talents wanted to be a part of UCLA. He not only taught success and won championships but he also showed how to live success through the values he stood for. Wooden found out what it took to be successful, made it his life's credo, and became inseparable from it. He eventually became the success he sought, and all those who came in contact with him knew that something very special was happening—that they were literally surrounding themselves with success.

The analogy to selling—and to life—is obvious. Success is not only repeating what works, it's an attitude—a winning attitude that can grow, mature, and grow some more as you learn from each new success. When you've made inroads persuading someone during your sales presentation, stop and think a minute: How did you treat your prospect; what did you say; how did you respond to his objections; what did you do to overcome rejection? If you can begin to fine-tune the answers to those questions, you're on your way to developing a successful, proven approach to selling that will pay dividends for years to come.

Enthusiasm Is Contagious

It's impossible to hear Zig Ziglar give a presentation without feeling tremendously enthusiastic. Master salesman and motivator, Ziglar has so much positive energy you'd swear he had just plugged himself into the nearest electrical outlet. That the great majority of those who hear him come away feeling genuinely inspired to change their sales or motivational approach is great testimony to the enthusiasm and love of his work he generates everywhere he goes. Like John Wooden, Zig Ziglar has become so involved with his work that he has become synonymous with it. Ziglar is fun. People believe selling can be fun. Ziglar is enthusiastic. People attack their selling with enthusiasm. Ziglar is filled with energy. People leave with their batteries recharged.

One of the most enthusiastic people I know is my mother-in-law. She greets us all with a smile, a bubbly laugh that says how much she enjoys life, and an intense interest in people that is pretty hard to match. Wherever she goes, she spreads enthusiasm about whatever is going on. Before you know it everyone around her has caught it, and the room is filled with energy. It is a quality that carries over to her work as a travel agent, and is one of the main reasons her services are so much in demand in her company.

Who are the enthusiastic people in your life? How long has it been since you have been truly enthusiastic about your sales efforts? Or, as Dr. Harold Blake Walker says:

> When was the last time you tried to punch a hole in the sky.... Test pilots, punching into the stratosphere, climbing to undreamed heights in jet and rocket planes, have a phrase they use to describe their work. They call it "punching holes in the sky." That is what we were meant to do with our lives, to climb beyond humdrum, reach up beyond preoccupation with gadgets and things, press on beyond "the little aims that end with self."[7]

So what if you've had some failures lately. Learn from them, and then forget them. It's a new day, yours for the winning. All you have to do is focus on all the positive aspects of your endeavors. Throw everything negative away. Think of all the opportunities that await you with a fresh, enthusiastic attitude. And although enthusiasm doesn't ensure success, remember that almost all successful people are enthusiastic. So attend lectures, enroll in classes, read self-improvement books (like this one), listen to motivational tapes, associate with upbeat, enthusiastic people, and very soon you will be spreading enthusiasm—and success—yourself.

Three

Prepare to Succeed—
and You Will!

Remember always, in the words of Pascal, that chance (or fortune) favors the prepared mind.

M. Lincoln Schuster

Control starts with planning. . . . Planning is bringing the future into the present so you can do something about it now.

Alan Lakein

It was happening to me, but it just couldn't be. The first night of the college play, the curtain scheduled to go up in less than two hours, and I didn't know my lines. How could I have gotten the dates wrong? And me with the lead in the play. I just didn't deserve it. As the minutes raced by and I managed to learn a few more lines, my mind couldn't help but think of all the misspent hours when I could have learned my part, but didn't—always finding something more important to do.

There was a knock on the door. "Five minutes, Mr. Somdal." My hands went clammy, my mouth felt like cotton, and my heart was pounding so wildly that I was sure the assembled audience could hear it. As I started through the door leading to the stage and my imminent acting debacle, I couldn't seem to remember even a single line of the few I had managed to memorize, my mind locking in on the enormous panic I was feeling. *Why didn't I prepare? Why didn't I study my lines? When will I ever learn?*

And then—thank goodness—I woke up. What an awful way to spend the night! It was the only nightmare I ever have (except when I eat pepperoni pizza), and in living color besides. I call it my "Ultimate Sales Nightmare," or "The *Real* Death of a Salesman." Because in sales, without adequate and accurate preparation, brother, you're finished.

This dream reappears every now and then—usually in times of heavy stress and overscheduling—because I know how important good preparation is in determining the final outcome of your persuasive presentation. And personally, I never want to be unprepared when going after a big account or into an important meeting. It can be unnerving, unproductive, and almost always unsuccessful.

What Do You Want to Accomplish— and Why?

Before you can begin to persuade someone to do something, you need to nail down your goal—that is, what it is you hope to accomplish. (More about the importance of goal setting later.) Sound elementary? It may seem simple, but it's surprising how many people just plunge in without stopping to think why they are where they are. It's the old "assemble the swing set, read the directions later" American way of doing things. And it can be extremely unproductive when it comes to sales.

I know a salesman who was having trouble making his quota. Neither he nor I could understand it. He was bright, dramatic, and extremely aggressive. He was making his calls, yet his sales run sheet was suffering. He was extremely frustrated and said, "I just don't know what's happening. I'm out there early every morning, take a half hour for lunch, and then stay late. I must have called on over twenty businesses today, and yet all I have is one ad to show for it. I'm really discouraged."

We went over everything he had done, and it all sounded right to me until a key phrase came from his mouth. "And then when I gave them their options of a half page or a full page, I was sure I would have at least some full pages, but I didn't get any. In fact, I only got one half page."

He was a new salesman, and he was going after small merchants to advertise in our newspaper. He was giving them some great sales arguments and terrific advantages to advertising. Yet when it came time to ask for the order, he was asking for an unrealistic initial advertising investment in proportion to the size of their company. He did not have the proper goal for the accounts he was pursuing. He wanted big ads because he wanted to succeed quickly and make his mark in the company. Did his customers realistically have the money to spend on the big ads? The answer, of course, was no. But because he had failed to successfully analyze in advance the size ad that could fit his potential customers' pocketbooks, he was largely unsuccessful in his efforts.

"Sell them one-quarter-page ads, at the largest," I said. "Get them to advertise in a smaller size, and with a greater frequency, and you'll not only make the income you would have from the larger sale, you'll keep them as satisfied customers for a long time, assuming the ads pull."

Eager to try a new approach, the salesman took my advice. He began to really look at the needs of each business instead of his own, and started to sell the way I knew he could. Today that salesman is one of the best in the company at analyzing his customers' budgets. Not uncoincidentally, he has one of the longest advertiser run sheets among our sales force, and it all started with recognition of this important point:

Analyze your prospect's needs—
and gear your presentation to meet them.

First Things First—Organization and Preparation

I have observed with amazement how little contemporary salesmanship books emphasize preparation before the attempted sale. Oh, there's a lot of the "show up on time, wear a clean, pressed suit" sort of advice for preparation before the sale (all of which has a good, sound basis) but very little in the way of strategic planning, organization, and goal setting. I think it's because most people are impulsive by nature and like to "get at it" without thinking very much about it. But just as in the case of my young sales friend, that can prove frustrating and disastrous. In my opinion the credo—and in some cases, the epitaph—of salespeople who do this continually certainly could be "Fools rush in. . . ."

Lest you think you are immune to this sort of thing, remember that even the best salesmen can have problems with organization and planning. The young Frank Bettger, phenomenally successful insurance salesman though he was, just couldn't seem to get himself organized. After setting a personal goal of two thousand new sales calls for the year, he fell so hopelessly behind that he stopped keeping records—until he thought about it and decided what he needed to do. He set aside Saturday morning and called it "self-organization day."

During this time, Bettger would do those essential things so necessary in the life of a successful salesman. He would plan his whole week, day by day, analyzing each call as to its particular problems and demands, figuring out different proposals for each one. This took several hours, but when Monday rolled around, Bettger was more organized than he had ever been before. Organization Saturday proved so successful that several years later he moved it to Friday morning, accomplishing the same amount of work in four and a half days that he had previously gotten done in five—all because he was organized and planned ahead, illustrating this essential point:

Planning doesn't waste your time—it saves your time.

Be Prepared to Negotiate on the Spot

Personally, I struggle with organization and have all my life. (Those who know me will hardly find this a news flash.) However, over the years I have learned to appreciate the value of adequate preparation and organization, especially during those critical moments when the sale is on the line, and something needs to be said quickly to persuade the prospect or at least get him to think in my direction again.

I had no idea that such a moment would enhance my future at the *Wave* less than a week after I started there. Although I had been hired as National Advertising Manager, I had retail advertising experience through my previous advertising agency affiliation. So it came as no surprise when my boss asked me to go on a retail sales call with one of the local salesmen, a man we shall call John. John had arranged a meeting with a very large retail furniture chain, which was somewhat amazing since we were a much smaller newspaper then and since the particular store involved was several miles out of our circulation area. But John had a certain feeling about this account, and in deference to his years in the business, we decided to go after it.

Prior to the meeting, I became as familiar as I could with my new company, and went over an advertising-rate strategy with John and my boss which we felt would help us get the account. (Basically, we were offering a low contract rate if we could be assured of a large volume of ads over a long period of time.)

Well, that was quite a meeting. The store manager was a tough, no-nonsense merchant, and his advertising manager was a sharp businesswoman who asked question after question about our paper. John was holding his own, and I would interject occasionally with the limited knowledge I had of my brand-new company.

After the rate presentation, which was the final part of the meeting, the office suddenly became quiet. To break the tension, I asked, "When do we begin your ad schedule?"

"Your rate's too high," said the tough boss. "Way too high." Again it was quiet. John began to perspire, and he laughed nervously. He really wanted the account and the pressure was enormous.

"No, it's not," I said quietly. "You're getting a tremendous rate, based on volume and frequency."

"I still think it's too high. I don't think we'll be able to do business. What do you think, Marie?"

Everyone turned to Marie, the advertising manager, who had shown signs of being every bit as tough as her boss, but who had remained quiet until now. She directed her attention to my associate and asked, "Will you absorb the plate cost?"

Knowing that the cost of the plate used in the printing process was nominal, I made a quick decision before my fellow salesman had a chance to speak.

"You bet we will," I said. "Assuming we get the same ad size and schedule we have been discussing."

After a long consultation, they both agreed and we were home free with the account. While we were waiting to take them to lunch, my associate nervously called me aside.

"How can you do that?" We don't have any authorization to give them a free plate for each ad. The boss isn't going to like this."

I'm happy to say, the boss not only liked it, he *loved* it. We got a huge account that we held onto for several years, all for the cost of a plate, which was practically inconsequential. What our *Wave* salesman didn't understand was what happened in that crucial moment when the prospect said the rate was too high. Neither one of us wanted to budge on the rate, but the dynamics of the situation *demanded* we concede something. It was a moment that cried out for a power selling point. That I knew the cost of the plate—or, that I was prepared to calculate the cost of the plate versus the income from the ad—and John, who should have had the knowledge, didn't, was the biggest difference between us on that day. And it proved to make the difference in getting the account, illustrating:

More product knowledge means more selling success.

You're in Control When You Plan

All of us would like to be in control when we're in a situation where we need to persuade someone to our point of view.

Adequate and accurate planning and preparation can help us achieve that control we so desire.

Just think about it for a minute. Preparation really isn't such hard work if you analyze all the activities with which you have been involved that meant something to you. If you really cared about your involvement and the eventual outcome, you probably prepared as much as you could prior to the event.

Everyone who has been a serious student knows how necessary it is to prepare in advance for a test. When my brother-in-law was in college, he was so prepared for his tests that he often went to the movies the night before, reasoning that if he didn't know the material at that late date, he never would. Asking the boss for a raise, going to an important job interview, and popping the question to your intended life partner are examples of important moments when most of us have had to be prepared.

It was New Year's Eve almost twenty years ago when a scared, nervous, and terribly excited young college man sat in a crowded restaurant across from the most wonderful, beautiful person to have ever come into his life. As he clutched the little ring box in his suit pocket, he did his best to make interesting conversation, belying the extreme case of nerves he felt at that moment (and the death grip he had on the little box). But at least, he thought, he was prepared, and as he launched into all of the differences he and his girlfriend had had over the previous two years, a sense of relief spread throughout his whole being. They were actually discussing points that had developed into disagreements in the preceding months. The difference was that no one had an ego to defend or a position to protect. And although his date was puzzled as to why they were discussing these things, she was as calm as he was in talking over the relatively few things they had ever argued about.

You can probably guess that the young man was me and the beautiful young woman sitting across the table was my girlfriend, and about to become my fiancée, after I asked the final and most important question of my survey: "Do you think we can settle our differences?" Twenty years later my wife and I still laugh about my "market research" approach to proposing to her. (Let me assure you that it was a memorable, romantic evening from that point on.)

I think we both learned something from that magic night: Each of us had a few doubts, small though they now seem, and by bringing up the issues that stood in our way and then discussing them, we were more able to be certain that it was a choice we could make with little or no reservations.

When to Plan

The first thing to know about preparation is that you should allow plenty of time to prepare. If what you are planning for is going to be worthwhile if you succeed, then by all means take some time and plan correctly. Otherwise you may find yourself rushing out of your office or your home, half-cocked, half-prepared—and destined to failure before you start.

For example, if you're in sales, you know when you're going to see certain accounts and what problems and special challenges each presents. So if you have an important meeting in three days, don't wait three days to prepare. Prepare *now!* If you give yourself more time to think, you'll be able to more thoroughly cover the objections to what it is you are trying to sell—and therefore, have a much greater chance to close the deal.

Hint: Planning—*adequate* planning—takes time. Why not try getting up half an hour earlier each morning, and devoting that half an hour to advance planning. You'll find that extra time will do wonders for your organization, your confidence, and ultimately, your success.

Set Goals Today for Success Tomorrow

Goal setting is one of the most important things that everyone, regardless of occupation, can do in their lives. In selling, however, I think it may be the *most* important thing. Good salesmen are constantly setting goals, and then qualifying and requalifying them. This week, how many calls can I make? Of those calls, what is my interview goal? And when all is said and done, will I reach my sales goal of xx dollars?

Salespeople basically have very little else to spur them on, except for pride in doing the best job possible. Successful, competitive salespeople keep score so they can know how well they are doing. Things like sales made and dollar-volume sold are often the only yardstick for measuring a salesperson's performance—other than the knowledge that he has done the best job he could do.

The salesman who sets his dollar or number of sales goal for himself, then sets off to achieve that goal through a series of related subgoals, will in all likelihood be more successful than the salesman who has nothing in his job to shoot for. Similarly, fund raisers, teachers, parents—anyone who needs to persuade others—will all stand a much better chance of succeeding if they have a clearly established goal in mind before they set out.

Why is that, you ask? The answer really lies in the nature of the beast. I've often felt that selling can on its most unproductive days be a lot like trying to nail Jell-O to a wall. You know where and what the stuff is and you've got your hands on it, but just when you're about ready to "nail down the sale," it slips out of your grasp.

Without a goal to pursue, even the best salesman among us can become discouraged and forget that sales is a numbers game. There will be a certain amount of *nos*, but those *no* answers get each salesman that much closer to the *yes* he's worked so hard to hear. So the rule for goal setting is a simple but important one:

Write your sales goals down, and review them often.

Remember: your goals are the result of your hard work. That you haven't reached them yet, and that you have yet to do the persuasive work necessary to accomplish them, is really irrelevant at this point. That you want to *achieve* your goals, and you *believe* you can, are the most important things about them. They are road maps for your future success, and you need to refer to them often to stay on course toward the sales achievements you've decided to pursue.

How Goal Setting Can Affect You at a Critical Moment

In sales, as in life, people can easily sidetrack you from achieving what you set out to accomplish. The number of distractions we all have in our busy lives is enormous, and the situation is no different in the office of the busy executive you're trying to sell. I've been interrupted in the middle of my sales presentations by office telephones, co-workers popping in and out, the arrival of the coffee truck, low-flying airplanes, window washers, and even a Saint Patrick's Day parade. A salesman trying to sell in the midst of any of these distractions still has the same obligation: to sell his product or service with his original goal in mind.

Even more difficult than the above distractions are those made by the prospect himself with regard to your product—especially if he brings up half a dozen different objections for not buying what you're selling, none of which seem to you to relate to what you have been talking to him about.

It is at this precise moment that your mind should click into overdrive and you should remember—after all those careful hours of preparation and organization—just what your goals are, as they relate to your prospect, and what it is you want to have him do. Often, you must force the issue and say something such as, "Getting back to the original point. . . ." Or, if your prospect has just made a point you have no hope of winning, you must think of a way of agreeing with him without compromising yourself, and then switch the subject back to the reason you came there in the first place. In other words:

Keep your prospect on track—and moving
toward agreement.

As a salesman, it is imperative that you spend most of the interview discussing your product or service and what it can do for your prospect, and that any changes in course be side-stepped or recharted in the right direction immediately. A final bit of preparation can help you accomplish this.

Analyze Your Prospect and His Company

If you've never met your prospect before, or have only talked with him on the telephone, there is very little you can do to find out what he is like before your first meeting. However, you can and should delve into his company. Ask yourself these questions: What do they want and need? Who are they? What will motivate them? And equally important, how will my product or service not only help my prospect's company but how will it also help make his job easier or at least no more complicated?

One of the most famous novelists in American literature used to do this kind of "biographical detective work" prior to and during the writing of each of his books. William Faulkner would develop a character sheet, upon which he would write everything he knew about that character. He would then take the collection of all of these sheets and tape them to the walls of his office all around him. They were then in plain sight for him to refer to whenever he was in doubt about a character's motivation or what he might do in certain situations.

If you are in a position to know what will motivate the particular person you are trying to persuade, so much the better. One of my favorite ministers at the church my wife and I attend once sent me a letter that I shall never forget. He was attempting to solicit my aid for a particular church project that promised to be difficult and occupy much of my time for several months to come. Knowing that I had just served on a committee and was tired, but also knowing that I was just as susceptible to a compliment as the next person (more so according to my wife), he sent me a letter that began this way:

> Dear Mike:
> The Lord needs five good men. . . .

Now I ask you, how can you turn down a request worded that way? He had done his homework, analyzed his prospect, and was truly prepared to succeed. In fact, of the first five men he solicited, all five attended the first meeting, with two of us eventually going on to form the committee that completed the project.

How well do you know your prospect and his business or environment? And have you got a handle on just what it is you hope to accomplish? Have you got an ultimate goal in mind? And finally, are you organized and prepared enough to stick to your goal—or to recall it during even the most animated discussion, complete with interruptions?

If you can answer all of these questions decisively and affirmatively, then you are truly prepared to persuade.

Four

Telemarketing:
Direct Line to More Sales

Since telemarketing is generally a "numbers game," results are in direct proportion to effort. With the proper dedication, even the poorest of salespeople can find success through telemarketing.

William J. McDermott

They think too little who talk too much.

Dryden

The thing that used to strike the most fear in my heart was when I would get home from a hard day's work, and my wife would say to me in a tone normally reserved for more solemn occasions (like funerals), "Honey, we just got the phone bill. But I'm not going to talk to you about it now, because I don't want to upset you."

Now, however, I am getting more resigned to having a phone bill that closely resembles the national debt. I'm not quite sure why this happens, but I do have a couple of wild hunches. One has to do with the fact that my wife is a member of several volunteer organizations (and no one seems to volunteer unless she calls them to let them know that they just have). The other hunch, though, really has more merit: We have teenagers.

I find it strange that while most teenagers treat this device as an absolute necessity (and it isn't), most businesses—while agreeing that the telephone *is* an absolute necessity—never seem to get past the adolescent years in their approach to its use. Even the invention of the supercharged word *telemarketing* hasn't seemed to help much. A rude, uncaring telephone manner, and being put on "terminal" hold, have become more the rule than the exception. And when it comes down to using the phone to sell or to gain a meeting for the purpose of persuading someone, many people who should know either have limited knowledge in how to use it effectively or are downright afraid to try it on a regular basis.

Encountering the Unseen Prospect

Of course, the difference here is between the known and the unknown—calling someone who is your friend and chatting amiably versus calling someone you've never met before. There can be a great deal of rejection waiting at the other end of the line, and it is often reason enough to postpone or put off entirely making an important telephone call. Maybe he (your prospect) has had a bad day . . . maybe you're interrupting a meeting ... the last three people you called were gruff and hung up on you—maybe he will, too ... you'll call him to-morrow. It's easy to become "call reluctant" and stop initiat-ing phone calls at all costs. And without an efficient regular use of the phone, that cost can be quite high: fewer opportunities to sell or persuade because of a failure to master the high-speed communicator of our day, the telephone.

The wife of a good friend of mine works part time in mar-keting research and has really become very good at what she does. But it wasn't always like that. In fact, when she first started, she was given a "terrible assignment" (in her words): she had to make cold telephone calls, interviewing people she had never met before with a survey that took a minimum of ten minutes. And even worse than that, she was instructed to make these calls at the two worst possible times: dinner time, and first thing in the morning.

"I can't do it," she said to her husband, staring at one of the blank questionnaires. "These people don't know me. Why would they want to talk to me? And especially at these times. I'll just call the office and quit."

Her husband reassured her that she could do a great job, that she was warm and friendly, and that the market research company had provided her with a script. "Come on. Give it a try. You'll be great." And give it a try she did, completing half a dozen surveys that very night. When her husband asked her what made the difference, she told him something that made a great deal of sense, and changed her whole way of looking at the project.

"On the first call, I told the man at the very beginning I hoped I wasn't interrupting his dinner, and that normally I would have called earlier or later, but I was given this precise time by my company to conduct the survey. Well, he was so nice! He thanked me for my courtesy, said that he didn't envy me my job, and he would be happy to answer the survey questions. I discovered at that moment that people are people, whether you talk to them face to face or over the phone. They all want to be treated with courtesy and respect, so by treating them that way and being sensitive to their potential inconvenience, I had very little trouble from that point on." Words of wisdom from a nonprofessional salesperson who learned more about relating to people on the phone in a short period of time than many salespeople do in a lifetime. Several years later, she now feels so comfortable on the phone that she says, confidently, "I work well on the telephone"—a far cry from the "I want to quit" stage. So, the rule for encountering the unseen prospect might be stated this way:

> *Relax—and treat your phone prospect with courtesy, respect, and sensitivity.*

Cold Calls Are Out—Warm Calls Are In

In my opinion, there really is no such thing as the "cold" telephone call. There is the "first" telephone call, or the "initial point of contact." But no cold phone call. It's just not a part of my vocabulary.

What mental image do you conjure up when you think of the "cold phone call?" Discomfort? Yes. A chilly reception? Positively.

Let's face it—cold calling has absolutely *nothing* going for it. Why would anyone in his right mind want to make a cold phone call, when all that's waiting for him on the other end of the line is bleakness, misery, and certain rejection? Therefore, I propose to make the following revolutionary change in sales jargon:

The cold call shall, from this point on,
be known as the warm call.

Now, don't you feel better already? No longer is your telephone call a chance for confrontation with a cold, uncaring person on the other end of the line. The fact is that it really never was. Then what's changed? You, and your attitude toward your phone opportunity. And to arrive at this new attitude (if you're not already there) all you have to do is remember these few simple points before you dial:

1. *You respect the other person's time, and let him know it.*
2. *You have information of great value to impart to your prospect, well worth his time.*
3. *You are organized, know what you want to accomplish, and get right to the heart of the matter.*
4. *You enjoy what you're doing.*
5. *You really like the human being on the other end of the line—until he proves you wrong, beyond a shadow of a doubt!*

Remember—you're the one who's calling. And although your prospect didn't ask or expect to be interrupted by you, allow him the opportunity to be a pleasant, warm individual. Given the opportunity, most people will really respond to someone who genuinely appears to have their best interests, and their time, at heart. The reward is that those people who follow these simple principles will have a lifetime of warm calls ahead of them, and the growing confidence of the people they are calling on.

Getting Past Telephone Defenses

If you're with me to this point but are still scratching your head about how to get past the prospect's secretary, relax.

You're not alone. Even the warmest of warm telephoners—including me—have trouble with this one. Corporate America's first line of defense is the telephone—or rather, the secretary on the other end of the telephone. You know the one: her boss (your prospect) is always in a meeting. Or he's "gone for the rest of the day." Sometimes you're amazed that she even remembers his name, because he never seems to be around.

Everyone—and I mean *everyone*—who is attempting to sell someone something gets this treatment sooner or later. Therefore, you must expect it and not be put off, discouraged, or offended by it. No one is rejecting you personally. You just haven't had a chance to be *accepted* yet. Believing that, here's how you proceed:

> *Plan the details of your phone call*
> *(and be nice to the prospect's secretary).*

Assuming that you are told that your prospect (we'll call him Mr. Jones) is not in, plan your responses accordingly. For example:

> Is Mr. Jones in? . . . May I speak to his secretary? . . .
> (then, talking to Jones's secretary) I think Mr. Jones will
> be very interested in what my company offers. Let me
> take just a minute to explain roughly what it's about, and
> then you can tell me if I have the right office.

In this brief exchange, the salesman has determined that (a) Jones is not in, (b) he is speaking directly with Jones's secretary—the person who gets paid to communicate with Jones, and (c) he has asked for the secretary's help, or opinion, on whether Jones is the right person to see. Although they are all important, this last point is key to this whole approach. The salesman made the secretary feel important, that she was truly a decision maker and could help him determine whether or not Jones was indeed the person he should see. He enlisted her aid, got her thinking his way, included her as part of his team. He didn't treat her abruptly, as many salespeople treat secretaries. Acknowledging her importance to her boss and her company, he adhered to this important rule:

Take the prospect's secretary into your confidence— and ask for her help.

If you think about it, there's really nothing very complex about this approach. There's something appealing about someone asking for your help or opinion. It says, "You and your work here really matter . . . your contribution is important." Try it with anyone who is not your primary interview source. You will find that you will be greatly appreciated wherever you go, and will often be able to transcend even the stiffest office barrier.

Important: Thank the secretary, no matter how helpful she's been (even if she hasn't been the slightest bit helpful, she has, after all, given you some of her valuable time). It could pay dividends later, for she will remember you as sincere and polite and just might pave the way for you to get in to see the elusive prospect in the future.

Don't Be Too Pushy

One last tip with regard to the secretary: Learn to recognize a busy, frustrated, tired, or harassed individual by the tone of her voice, and then immediately play to the feeling you sense in the secretary before you get to the point of your message. In other words, treat her as a human being. For example:

"I know it's late in the day, and you must be very tired, but . . ."

"I really appreciate your carrying my message to Mr. Jones."

"You must have the busiest phone in the whole office, so I won't impose unduly on your time."

"I've been trying to catch up with Mr. Jones all day. I hate to disturb you, but . . ."

The principle is a fundamental one: Recognize the secretary's importance as a human being first, then as a secretary, and in most cases you will build a valuable contact and friendship.

When You Get Through to the Prospect

Anyone who finally manages to get through to his prospect should know what it is that he or she wants to say. As fundamental as this may seem, it is more difficult to do than it appears. It can be especially difficult if you are the one who has to recruit more members for your committee, raise funds for your church, or convince someone to change car pool days with you. Whether or not your profession is selling, one truth about answering the phone remains: It takes all of us away from whatever we were doing at the time, so the person attempting to persuade should get to the point quickly.

I think everyone can learn from watching how a good, professional salesman operates quickly and effectively on the telephone. His goal is to gain an interview, and his presentation might go something like this:

Hello, Mr. Jones, I appreciate your time, so I'll be brief [polite, disarming]. My name is [your name] with the

[company name] and I've got an idea for your company
you're going to love. Here's why: It will generate more
business in a shorter period of time and at a very small or
negligible overall cost [establish profit interest and cost
advantage for the prospect]. Rather than spend your time
on the phone [thoughtful], I can briefly outline what it's
about, and then set up a meeting that would be convenient for both of us to discuss it more fully. [By telling
the prospect you're only going to take a short amount of
time, you tell him you're respecting his time and setting him at ease. You have freed yourself to extend that
time by a few precious seconds or even a minute or more
if the prospect is interested enough to engage you in
conversation.]

Two very important things have happened in this brief exchange: (1) the salesman has acknowledged that he has taken
time out of the busy prospect's day, and has thanked him for
it, and (2) the salesman has very clearly established the importance of his call—the fact that he has a way of showing Jones
how to generate more business in a shorter period of time at a
lower cost. Just like that, this potential business annoyance has
become a business conversation worth pursuing. Therefore,
the next rule for learning how to use the phone effectively is:

**Work to turn the telephone intrusion into
the prospect's opportunity.**

Apply this rule to situations in your own life and see how
logical it really is. At our house, when I'm home in the evening, the phone must ring at least fifteen times between the
hours of six and nine o'clock. And it's *never* for me. (Remember . . . we have teenagers.) Since I use the phone so much
during the day, the family knows that I actually prefer my telephone anonymity, and am really surprised when I do get a call

at home. And I must admit that, except for my friends, I almost always view these interruptions as an intrusion on my privacy. Therefore, whoever calls me selling something had better get to the point quickly and establish some interest for me or I'm going to hang up.

And that's just what happened one evening while I was working on this book. The phone rang just before nine o'clock and I answered it, convinced that I was just going to take another message. But the lady on the other end of the line actually asked for me. Not having been bothered by so much as a magazine salesman in the last three months, I really perked up and said, "Yes, this is Mr. Somdal." She identified herself and wanted to know if I had received the special package she had sent from her company.

I said, "What special package?" (the magic words, as it turned out). She was surprised I hadn't received it, and a little chagrined—genuinely, I thought—and added that it was all about a complete financial planning service that her company offered for busy executives like me. Of course I like to think of myself as a busy executive, so I was flattered. And because my wife and I had just been discussing how to pay for our daughter's college education, whether or not to make a certain investment we were considering, and how to better manage our cash flow *that very morning,* the call was certainly timely.

"I'm interested," I said. "Tell me about it."

"I really don't want to take your time on the phone, Mr. Somdal. And it does require at least twenty minutes. I'd love to set up an appointment, though. Would it be more convenient if I spoke with you at home or your office?"

Here I was, old "hang up on 'em" Somdal, actually being maneuvered into a choice of which meeting I wanted—not whether I even wanted one at all. But by this time, I was sold on at least hearing what she had to say. Timing certainly played a part in it because of my interest in the very subject she called about. But the way she handled herself from the beginning, with concern over whether I had received something she had mailed to me, her perceived understanding of what my needs might be, and her professionalism in handling the questions I put to her and in setting up an appointment, were all points of the presentation that gave her an *A* in this particular "warm" phone call.

When the Going Gets Tough

There will be those times when you can't get a meeting, no matter what. But in those cases, you should always leave yourself an opening to some other course of action.

For example, "In deference to your time, I'll send you some materials on our proposal, then follow it up with a phone call." Or, "This really seems to be a busy time for you. How about if I call you again in a week and a half?"

You should always—always—leave yourself an opening to come back and fight another day. Some people are just going to turn you down. If everyone said yes, the world would very quickly be full of sellers and no buyers. If you have the right product or service, and if you have time enough to sell it, there will be time enough to come back and *change your prospect's mind.*

The Ultimate Challenge

Having said that, there are times when you can turn the corner on an obstacle and change someone's thinking. I call this the "art of the three Ps—be *practical, persistent,* and *pertinent.*"

For in the art of telephone persuasion, if you can learn to recognize a definite no and a tentative no, you'll be miles ahead in how you approach each customer. The definite no is pretty easy to spot—he's cold, quick, and has a voice like a dial tone.

The tentative no, on the other hand, is a little more slippery. The door is always left open, if even slightly. For example, "I'm really busy this week." Or, "The budget won't be reviewed for another month." And, "Why don't you send me something in the mail." This is what I call a "No, but . . ."

A word of clarification: The yes and the definite no answers occur least often, so it's really essential for you to learn how to deal with the "No, but . . ." kind of response. A professional salesman might respond to such a vague kind of no in the following way:

> Mr. Jones, I really appreciate your doubts and concerns. I might have them myself if I were in your place. But believe me, I don't want to waste your time any more than you want to waste mine. I make my living selling, and I pride myself on how well I qualify each prospect before I call. Based on [summarize two or three strong needs he has that your proposal will satisfy], you are extremely well qualified to benefit from what my company offers. But neither you nor I will ever know if I'm right until I can have a few minutes of your time to show you what I mean. [Here comes the gutsy part.] Now, Mr. Jones, if I can't show you what I'm saying is true inside of ten minutes in your office, you won't have to put up with me again.

The salesman has been practical—he has condensed the reason he called to showing how his company can fulfill two or three of the prime needs of the prospect. It is obvious that he has been extremely persistent. And by challenging the prospect that he will not intrude on him any further if he doesn't interest him during a brief ten-minute visit, he has certainly been pertinent.

There is a fourth *P* to this approach—and that is Power, with a capital *P!* For at a critical juncture of the phone encounter, the salesman has emerged as a person who believes in himself and in what he is selling. He has bridged any credibility gap the unseen prospect may have built up about him through the strength of his convictions, his forthrightness, and his willingness to lay everything on the line.

In a moment, he has used real personal power to establish himself as important, and someone worth listening to, instead of just another salesman peddling something the prospect has no use for. He has given definite signals to the prospect that (a) his offer is worth considering, (b) he knows what he's talking about, and (c) ten minutes is really no gamble at all. Our last rule, then, for effective telephone persuasion is this:

Have enough faith in yourself and your product to challenge your prospect with how important it will be for him to meet with you.

How do you view the telephone? As an annoyance . . . with grudging acceptance because you really don't know how to effectively use it . . . as a cold, uncaring machine that transforms people into unfeeling monsters who hang up on you? Or do you look positively at this master of modern business convenience? Do you constantly work at trying to improve your telephone techniques? Can you hardly wait to get to the nearest phone to make a series of calls you know will help you sell your product or service? How you answer these questions can help determine your future selling success, or even whether or not you'll stay in sales, because the telephone will only continue to grow in importance and use, while salesmen who ignore its potential will fall by the wayside and become fond memories of the way things used to be done.

PART II

GO FOR THE SALE
EARLY AND OFTEN

Five

Winning From the Beginning

If you train your mind to search for the positive things about other people, you will be surprised at how many good things you can observe in them and comment upon.

Dr. Alan Loy McGinnis

The only way to have a friend is to be one.

Emerson

During my first few months at the *Wave*, I was actively pursuing an account with a large major retail department store just a few doors away from my office.

To say that we were experiencing little success with this account would be a gross understatement. We received an occasional ad, but I knew our paper should really be getting a much heavier ad schedule from them. We had elicited little interest from the company, and had not been able to meet with the advertising manager for a variety of reasons.

To make matters worse, we just couldn't seem to get a paper delivered to the store manager, although his store was just half a block from my office. And even though our main office was the center for dispatching and was several miles away (I was located in our branch office at the time), he always seemed to call my office, naturally assuming I was in charge and could straighten out the problem. On the rare weeks when his company placed one of its ads in our paper, he would really get irate when he didn't receive a copy, something which seemed to happen to him and to no other customers.

After several instances of the same complaint, I decided that, for whatever reason, this must have been one of those snakebitten situations that just wasn't going to get any better unless something different was done. The store manager should have been an ally—someone as interested in seeing more of his company's ads in our paper as I was. Instead, he was fast becoming an adversary through a problem that really should never have happened once, let alone several times.

So, knowing that I would not only have to correct the problem but also change his impression of our company—no small task at that point—I set out to see what I personally could do. Early on publication day, I got a copy of our newspaper (his company did not have an ad in this particular edition) and walked the short distance down to his store, arriving just as it opened. Convinced that I had to see him personally, I told his secretary I just wanted to make sure he got a copy of the paper, and to say hello to him.

Let me tell you that was a positively frigid first meeting. He vented all of his frustration over why our dispatch department couldn't ever seem to get him his paper on time. Then, in a voice heavy with sarcasm, he thanked me for my concern and went right back into his office.

At this point, there was a great temptation on my part to make more out of my little public relations effort than it really was. As I walked back to my office, I thought—hoped, really—that the problem might be solved, and I could turn it over to my dispatch department again.

But I knew I just couldn't do that. Even though we would probably get him his paper close to 100 percent of the time from then on, he had extremely negative impressions of our company, and a longer-term approach was needed.

The plan was really very simple. I would spend a couple of minutes of my time each delivery day and personally hand deliver his paper to him. In the process (no matter how long it took), I was determined to get to know this man—it seemed like an impossibility at the time—and even become his friend if I could.

As the weeks went by, the barriers began to come down and a relationship developed during the one or two minutes we talked as I handed him his personally delivered paper. About the fifth or sixth week, he joked that I "must be the most expensive dispatcher on the *Wave*'s staff." By the time the eighth week rolled around, I was able to take him to lunch, where we discussed ways to improve his store and gain new customers through an expanded advertising schedule in our newspaper. The early problems faded from his memory, and we actually became good friends, getting our families together on a number of occasions and having lunch whenever possible.

In case you're wondering, yes, I finally stopped hand delivering his copy of the *Wave* every week, but only after several months of faithfully walking the short distance to his store each delivery day, spending the few minutes it took to seek him out, give him his paper, and walk back to my office again.

Those weekly moments, although extremely brief points of contact, allowed us to become better business acquaintances and, ultimately, friends, all of which resulted in more advertising from his company for our newspaper and more results for his store because of the additional ads.

In summary: Whatever the selling situation may be—whether it's an extreme problem, such as the one I faced, or merely the continuing challenge of constantly having to meet and persuade new people, remember this principle:

Take the friendship offensive immediately.

The kind of friendship I established with my manager friend was a solid, sustaining one. But it didn't just happen. I took the offensive and helped to make it happen. True, I was solving a sales problem at the time. But in the course of doing that, I made a good and solid friendship because I showed care, concern, and interest. And most important, I didn't just wait for something to happen. I took the initiative and made something very positive happen. It's a process that anyone who cares about other people willingly goes through, no matter how long it may take.

My close friend Dr. Alan Loy McGinnis built a bestseller around this principle in his first book, *The Friendship Factor.* This magnificent book is filled with ways to get closer to people, documented by McGinnis's extensive research into the subject. As he says:

> In research at our clinic, my colleagues and I have discovered that friendship is the springboard to every other love. Friendships spill over into the other important relationships of life. People with no friends usually have a diminished capacity for sustaining any kind of love. They

tend to go through a succession of marriages, be estranged from various family members, and have trouble getting along at work. On the other hand, those who learn how to love their friends tend to make long and fulfilling marriages, get along well with the people at work, and enjoy their children.[1]

What McGinnis seems to be saying is that those people who are successful in their friendships—and also in many other important interpersonal aspects of their lives—really work at becoming a friend. They take an active interest in others, and aren't concerned about the possible risks of rejection as they put their personality out on a limb for the sake of new friendship.

Show Your Prospect You Care About Him as a Person

Most important, however, is this rule regarding friendship: If you are truly interested in people and in establishing meaningful friendships (and any salesman who wants to succeed should be), you must show genuine warmth, and that you really care about the other person and his or her concerns. A calculating and manipulative friend is no friend at all.

Put another way, the professional salesperson or persuader who is out to become someone's friend for what he can sell him or get out of him is doomed to failure. He may get the order in the short run, and become the richest salesman in the company. But in the end, he will find himself bereft of real friends and bankrupt of spirit, a phony to even his best customers.

Let's look at the positive side of the equation in a direct-selling situation—at someone who demonstrated genuine warmth and really had his prospect's best interests at heart.

We are currently thinking seriously about buying another house. We have never had a view, and the view from our prospective new house is breathtaking (just as the ad said). The area and the house appear to be everything my wife and I ever wanted in a home. Combined with the fact that interest rates are dropping steadily, this seemed to be the time to make the move. And yet, there were lingering doubts. Should we even submit an offer? Are we moving just to satisfy my "annual rite of spring" (house hunting)? Why leave a home we had made so cozy and warm? And on and on. Whoever really wants to move from a place they've called home for several years, anyway?

And yet, somehow, here we were in the real estate office, with our friend who had just reentered the real estate business and had shown us the house. We were to meet her boss at 9:30 A.M. sharp, and he was going to take us through the offer we were to make, while our friend became reacquainted with the business.

After her boss, whose name was Ron, had kept us waiting for over an hour, I began to think that I should really get to my office, and that maybe this "once in a lifetime" house would have to wait until another day. Yet I kept my feelings to myself and sat down with my wife to begin to write out the contract.

What happened next was truly heartwarming, and renewed my faith in my profession. When we got to the part about length of escrow and selling the house we already own, Ron took off his glasses, stopped writing, and looked squarely at my wife and me.

"Are you prepared to carry two houses?" Ron asked.

"I don't think I'll have to," was my reply. "I plan to put mine up for sale if the bank accepts my offer."

"Let me tell you about someone who lives in your neighborhood. He had the same model house you own, and he bought another in the ranch section that was being built. He thought he had plenty of time to sell his house, but weeks turned into months, and before he knew it, his new house was ready and he hadn't sold the old one. He tried to carry both houses for a while but finally fell hopelessly behind in his new house payments, and the bank foreclosed."

"What happened to him?" I asked.

"The financial strain was so great that he and his wife started quarreling, and they finally got a divorce. She just moved out with the kids, and left him all alone in the house he could never sell. The point to all of this is that I don't want to sell you something that might do you more harm than good, by getting you boxed into an impossible situation."

Absolutely amazing! A real estate salesman who stood to make a big commission was actually spending several minutes to make sure we had carefully assessed all financial aspects of the situation. He was conveying genuine warmth and real caring, and he won two friends in my wife and me at that moment.

As I assured him we knew what we were doing and thanked him for his concern, my hope for the noble art of salesmanship was renewed. In his brief but powerful moment of caring, Ron had overcome not only his original tardiness (for which he apologized profusely) but even more impressively, he risked rejection by putting his true feelings out on a limb for us, and actually showed us the down side of what we were doing. In just a short period of time, he cemented our relationship, gave me great confidence in his skill and sales ability, and illustrated another key principle:

Show an interest in the other person's agenda.

After we finished the offer, our newfound broker friend asked all of us in the room if we could join hands and pray. We submitted the offer that night. It was truly a great day, made especially memorable because a salesman we had never met before had gone out of his way to show care, concern, and love for complete strangers.

Know When to Speak—and the Value of Just Listening

Anyone who has ever met Fulton Lytle and engaged him in conversation leaves him feeling as though something special had just occurred. And in reality, after a talk with this fine Presbyterian minister, something special does transpire. Fulton listens—I mean, really listens—to every word you're saying. His whole being, focused through his eyes, is intent on what you're saying, giving you the impression that at that moment, you are the most important person in the world to Fulton Lytle. And indeed, you are! For as long as I have known him, and probably for his entire life, Fulton has put the cares and concerns of other people before his own. And the results are apparent in his successful ministry, his full life, and his countless friends.

One of the leading life insurance salesmen in the world, Joe Gandolfo, recognized early in his career the great value of respecting your prospect's agenda, and listening to what he has to say. According to Joe:

> Too many salesmen bombard the client with conversation just because he pauses for a moment. That will often break his train of thought and possibly offend him. You have to remember that a man's voice is one of the great-

est sounds in the world to him, so let him talk when he wants to. There's no way you can be genuinely interested in him if you don't listen to what he's saying.[2]

There's no doubt about it. Conveying genuine warmth, concern, and interest in another person during a conversation takes concentration and large doses of willpower to refrain from jumping in with your own "wonderful, one-of-a-kind thought." But it can be done. And if you're a salesman, it *must* be done—right from the very beginning. Just remember to practice a few simple principles, and you'll be headed for success in the art of conveying genuine caring and interest in your prospect: When carrying on a conversation:

1. *Stay as still as you can.*
2. *Concentrate intently on what your prospect is saying.*
3. *Maintain eye contact.*
4. *Make sure you pause before jumping in, to allow your prospect time to finish.*

These few simple precepts can, with practice, greatly enhance your ability to relate to people, understand their needs, and in turn, give you the ability to answer those needs with the product, service, or idea you are attempting to sell.

Make the Most of Your Opening Minutes

Keith Hanson is not only a friend but also one of the leading real estate salespeople in Ventura County. I didn't realize how good a salesperson he was when I called him that first day a couple of years ago. I was looking for a small rental property to buy as an investment in the California beach city of Oxnard, not far from where we live. I had combed the real estate ads in the local area newspapers, and had made several phone calls to realtors inquiring about the property that was listed. My goal was not only to buy property but also to find a realtor with whom I could work on other property acquisitions in the coming years. After a solid morning of calling, I was thoroughly frustrated because no single realtor seemed to understand that I had different reasons for buying—investor reasons as opposed to owner-occupied reasons. There is a world of difference, but none of the so-called experts I called seemed to know it.

Wearily, I picked up the phone for what I vowed would be the last time that day, since it was already late in the afternoon and I was really discouraged at this point from the great lack of knowledge possessed by the realtors with whom I had spoken.

What a happy surprise when after only a minute or so of discussion with this last realtor, he asked, "If I hear you correctly, you're interested in this property from an investor's viewpoint, is that right?"

"Yes, that's absolutely correct," I said, as hope that I found someone who actually understood what I needed began to fill my spirits like helium.

"I deal with many investors who have discovered that Oxnard is really a growing area. Let me run this property you inquired about on the computer, and give you some numbers that you're probably very interested in. It will only take a minute."

I was astounded! The entire real estate fraternity in the city of Oxnard didn't seem to understand or care about my specific needs, and all of a sudden I was talking to a man who not only understood but also had a computer to help further analyze my needs.

This was just the start of my relationship with Keith Hanson, a relationship that has developed into a solid friendship and proven profitable for all concerned. I decided to buy from Keith because of his understanding of what I wanted and needed in the beginning few minutes of our relationship. He clearly established himself as someone who listened carefully to me and responded out of *my* agenda, not his. That Keith is the leading salesman in his company is no surprise to me. People will flock to someone who displays a genuine interest in them and puts them first at all times. Keith Hanson does that consistently and is rewarded with a long list of satisfied customers who come back to him whenever they have property they want to buy or sell. Keith understood and practiced a key sales point worth reiterating here:

> *When you first meet your prospect,*
> *listen carefully to his stated needs.*

It's really easy to understand. The idea of making a good first impression is something all of us are concerned with at one time or another, whether or not we're selling anything. From adolescence and the monumental importance of our first date, to the impression most people are obsessed with making on a job interview, we are all involved at important times in our lives with getting people to like us, with selling ourselves. And like it or not, those first few minutes can make or break the presentation.

Learn to Work With Your Available Material

My good friend and neighbor Ray Zoref is vice-president and partner of his own very successful furniture-manufacturing company. When I asked him if he remembered the most powerful beginning in any of his selling situations, he responded with this example:

"I remember when I was selling furniture for a national manufacturer, calling on retail furniture stores to get them to buy our product. The business was unbelievably competitive, and I was struggling a bit, until the company came out with a special promotion. Reasoning that color ads sell furniture better than black-and-white ads, they designed a full-color flyer showing their hottest selling furniture lines, printed thousands of them, and then gave large quantities to all of their salesmen for their accounts.

"The really unbelievable part," recalled Ray with a smile, "was that the company didn't want us to give the flyers away. We were supposed to sell them to the stores so that they in turn could mail them to their customers. Since nothing like this had been tried before, many of our salesmen failed because they couldn't believe it would work. They were furniture salesmen, not printing salesmen. The grumbling was long and loud. But for some reason, I saw it as a great challenge."

Knowing that he had a complicated proposal to sell, and realizing that he would have to get to the payoff quickly, he devised a short, simple, but powerful approach that gave him a winning beginning.

He began with a powerful question no one could disagree with: "How would you like to have the best February you've ever had?"

After the prospect agreed (nobody ever said no), Zoref proceeded to clinch the sale this way: "My business isn't selling circulars, it's selling furniture. It's your business, too. But this circular will help us both achieve our goals, to a greater degree than we had ever imagined possible." He then went into how color furniture ads always pulled more results, giving statistical proof and testimonials.

His results astounded even him. "I sold more circulars and more furniture than anyone else in the company during that period," Zoref recalled. "I believed in the promotion, and thought of a dramatic way to show that right at the start of my presentation. And because of my sincerity and conviction in the product, the rest came fairly easily. Not everyone had their best February, but almost everyone to whom I sold did significantly greater business than they thought they would. I solidified my relationships with many of my accounts, and took home a nice commission check at the same time."

Forgettable Openings

A section on how to open your presentation wouldn't be complete without a brief comment or two on what *not* to do. All of us have been approached by salespeople who exhibit all the sensitivity of a slug (that may be giving those charming little garden pests the worst of it).

You know the type: hard-nosed, hard-voiced, all mouth, no ears. They descend on you in the department store or the automobile showroom before you know it, and refuse to give you space (Tom Hopkins calls it "The Vulture Swoop."[3]) Or, they're the kind of salespeople who drone on and on and on, telling you every joke they ever knew, none of which are funny. You can only stop and marvel at their amazing breath control. They come in many sizes and shapes, in person or over the phone. But they all share one thing in common: they are extremely offensive to most people, and their chances of making a sale are greatly diminished. (Like the life insurance salesman who started every presentation by placing a small coffin on the prospect's coffee table.)

These hard-sell salespeople have been too concerned with their own success, their own values and agendas, to worry about the needs and feelings of the people whom they are supposed to be helping.

Lose Your Losers First (Dismiss Weaknesses Early)

If you play pinochle at all, you know the old saying: lose your losers first. In some ways selling is not unlike this popular card game. Far better for you to come thundering down the stretch to your summary and know there are no barriers to the finish line, than trip and fall over some minor objection you never really answered earlier.

Specifically, if your presentation or your company has an Achilles' heel, and you know your prospect is as aware of it as you are, by all means bring it up (although your natural tendency might be to overlook it). You should be fully prepared to discuss any weakness in your plan or program, and then be equally prepared to refute the argument with your own solid, well-thought-out argument.

A word of caution: This can be risky business if you are not thoroughly knowledgeable of all the facts of the matter—but far riskier if you don't say anything and assume the problem will disappear all by itself.

What does it take to win from the beginning? Nothing less than a totally organized, beautifully prepared presentation, filled with strong opening statements. This is not difficult if you work at it, and most importantly, you'll know that if you can accomplish this consistently, you are destined to win your share of persuasive presentations.

Six

Compare—Compete— and Convince

It goes without saying that a thorough knowledge of competing propositions must underlie any such effort to eliminate them.

Richard Buskirk

Selling can be the loneliest profession in the world. Professional salespeople receive regular doses of rejection every day of their selling lives. It goes with the territory—rejection, discouragement, frustration, and often a feeling that one will never again recapture the ability to sell or persuade people.

These are the times that "separate the men from the boys," the above-average salespeople from those who will never gain the status, income, or job satisfaction they thought selling would give them. What on earth do you do when this truth dawns on you? The possible responses vary widely: Give up altogether. Figure out the company and the system, and then sell just enough to keep your job, never looking beyond your nose or the company water cooler to see just how great your future could be. Or, worse yet, never ask for or look for help, sinking further and further into an abyss of nonproduction and self-doubt, until eventually you lose the job which you haven't been able to do for the last weeks or months anyway.

The truly great salespeople respond in another way. They find out what it takes to rise out of the doldrums, to be great in their field. What they do is simple enough but requires some effort, something most people aren't willing to give. Let's face it: It's a lot more comfortable to come home after a hard day at the office than go to a seminar on how to improve your selling. Who among us takes the time and energy to register for a night class with a twelve-week commitment, just so we can improve in our profession? These levels of dedication are never reached by most salespeople, yet it is precisely this kind of approach that can make the difference between success and failure, between mediocrity and the ability to rise above the average.

Use the Successes of Others as Inspiration

When the going gets tough, ask yourself this question: How do the successful people do it? Why is he able to get volunteers for his organization so easily, while I seem to struggle with it constantly? If So-and-So can make a six-figure income, why can't I? These are legitimate questions, and the answers can provide a real key to success in selling. That you can become what you believe is as real today as it ever was, and is illustrated time after time in successful selling organizations all across the country.

In his new book, *Bringing Out the Best in People*, Dr. Alan Loy McGinnis illustrates just how true this principle is in the chapter called "The Power of the Success Story." McGinnis says, "When our leader exposes us to successful people, it not only inculcates certain values, it also convinces us that if they can achieve, so can we. Seeing another succeed somehow inspires us to succeed."

McGinnis goes on to show how this principle works in the highly successful Mary Kay Ash cosmetics organization, a company with a phenomenal growth rate and success story achieved in just a few short years.

> If you visit a meeting of the Mary Kay organization you will see this principle applied again and again. A crowd of people will sit in rapt attention hour after hour and get more inspired simply by listening to success stories. The motivational technique is really quite simple. People walk up to the microphone and recount their struggles and their triumphs. The message sounds like a refrain: "If we did it, you can do it too." They show slides of their new homes and luxury cars, and they tell basically the same story: "We came from nothing. You can do the same thing simply by believing hard enough and working hard enough." [1]

The inspirations are all around you if you just look for them. And whatever degree of fame or fortune those people may have achieved, the lessons to be learned are the same: The people in my profession have achieved success, so why can't I? The answer is clear: You can be successful in selling and give yourself a big boost by comparing your efforts with others in your field or in your own office. What did they do, how did they do it, and why, are questions that can be answered with study, patience, and perseverance.

One of the greatest models for me in my early selling days was my boss and mentor, Larry Hews, who taught me the real value of perseverance in the field of newspaper advertising sales. Time and again, I would watch him come back from sales presentations to a new account rejected, but never discouraged. There was always a new way to approach the account, something new to try, always another day to sell. And although I'm extremely competitive and hate to quit until "the last dog is dead," there are many times I think I would have were it not for this outstanding example of patience and perseverance which I saw at work every day. The lesson I learned was this:

Compare your efforts with the successes in your field.

It's Never Too Late to Succeed

One of the healthiest things about comparing yourself to other successful people is that success has no age limit. Everybody's clocks are different. Class reunions are great for keeping this in perspective. Remember the football hero you knew you could never be like, and who now has gained one hundred pounds and is nowhere close to being the hero you idealized? But even better, doesn't it give you a real shot in the arm to discover the class ugly duckling has become a beautiful, poised, and successful person you never would have known if you hadn't read the name tag?

There are many notable examples of people achieving success very late in life. Colonel Harland Sanders didn't open his first Kentucky Fried Chicken restaurant until he was past his retirement years. Grandma Moses and her now-famous primitive art career didn't get started until she was well past rocking-chair age.

And the late Ray Kroc, founder of the unparalleled fast-food success, McDonald's, didn't begin his company until the age of fifty-two. Denis Waitley, prominent author and lecturer, chronicles this success in his best-selling book *Seeds of Greatness*:

> Ray Kroc of McDonald's is a classic example of an individual who never gave up on his dream. He really didn't hit his stride until he was 52. He began selling paper cups and playing the piano part-time to support his family in the early 1920s. After seventeen years with Lily Tulip Cup Company he became one of the company's top salesmen. But he gave up security with the company and struck out on his own in the milk shake business. . . . The most important message in the McDonald's story, I think, is that although Ray Kroc paid his dues as a salesman and didn't begin his new business until he was 52, he was able to build McDonald's into a billion dollar business in twenty-two years! It took IBM forty-six years to reach one billion dollars in revenues, and Xerox sixty-three years.[2]

When you are in doubt, and nothing seems to be working, remember that in selling, nothing comes easy. Those who have made a success of selling or promoting a product or service have done it with dedication and hard work. Perseverance is a commonly used word, but it applies here. Add this very simple fact to the whole equation:

If others succeeded in your field, you can, too.

By comparing yourself with winners, instead of dwelling on the setbacks that must come to us all, you are one giant step ahead in your attitude, and that much closer to being the success you want to be.

Compare Your Efforts With the Competition

As much as anyone selling needs to compare his efforts with
others in times of difficulty to keep the situation in perspective,
it is just as important—maybe even more so—to keep track of
the competition on a regular basis.

The key, once again, is proven success—case histories you
can study. How are the other guys doing? Are they getting
more of the business than I am? If so, why? What are they
doing that I'm not? These are questions that should always be
of concern to you, especially if you are a professional salesperson, because believe me, your competition is watching *you*
like a hawk.

If you don't take this position, and think that if you "build a
better mousetrap, the world will beat a path to your door," you
have subscribed to a belief that is only partially true. In light of
today's intense competition in all areas, this well-worn phrase
should be rewritten to read: "Build a better mousetrap, and the
world and all the mousetrap makers will beat a path to your
door."

Without going into all the political and social ramifications
of fierce competition from abroad, it is safe to say that you and
I—whatever selling situation we may find ourselves in—will
face competition from someone or some organization who
wants the business we are pursuing just as badly as we do.

Facing this inevitability and knowing how to deal with it
are, unfortunately, two different things. "I ignore the competition" is a refrain I hear all too often from salespeople who
should know better. "I just concentrate on *my* product," these
blasé salespeople say, "because it really sells itself. I don't have
to worry about competition, because there is none." To say
that this view is unenlightened is an understatement. Ignoring
the competition merely invites it to get your part of the busi-

ness it always wanted. But to acknowledge its existence, and then arm yourself to face it wherever you must, can only serve to enhance your market intelligence, product knowledge, and ultimately, your chances of closing the sale. Summarized, this point is well worth noting:

Study the competition—it's only smart.

Competition in selling is not a subject that is often addressed in books on selling. In the books on salesmanship I have read, nobody seems to focus on or even mention the value of knowing your competition, let alone how to deal with it. However, its importance and the extent to which major corporations place value on knowing their competition cannot be overemphasized. In a recent feature article, *Fortune* magazine stated what has become the corporate position on competition:

> Businessmen believe competition has intensified and become global. In industries where growth has slowed, executives realize that most of the increased business they need will have to come out of the hides of their competitors. . . . Companies realize that, without taking the behavior of competitors into account, their strategic plans don't work.[3]

While most people certainly don't want to take anything out of their competitors "hides," at the same time almost everyone would agree that they would rather not see the competition get a jump on them. For many salespeople who don't know how to cope, worry is the only answer. But for others who have learned the value of staying competitively sharp, there are ways of "fighting" the competition that tend to hone all of their sales skills—and can help to turn around a selling situation just in time.

Proceed Carefully When Referring
to the Competition

When asked to compare his furniture line with his major competitor's by a very interested furniture store, the salesman didn't miss a beat and thought he was giving a perfect answer. "Well, you and I both know Ray. He's a terrific guy, and he's been in the business a long time. But you know, his line is pretty inferior."

As my friend, furniture manufacturer Ray Zoref, was telling me this story, I remarked at how clearly it stood out in his mind although it had happened some twelve years before. "I'll tell you why," said Ray. "That story is as clear to me today as it was when it happened because of how off base the salesman competing against me was. The client told me the story with great relish, and finished it by saying he would never buy another stick of furniture from that man. And the reason was simply that he had chosen to run down my line through his opinion and innuendo. The fact that he had tried to build me up as a nice guy before he attacked my company was even worse in the eyes of the retailer. It was simply a transparent character and company assassination with absolutely no concrete facts or figures to back up what he was saying. And as far as the client was concerned, he didn't want to deal with someone on a regular basis who more closely resembled a shark than a human being."

What is even more surprising than the story and the point it illustrates is how often this kind of attack occurs. And the thing to understand here is that we are talking about *attack*, not a focus on what the competition does and how your product or service compares. In a situation like this, there's a basic principle of human nature at work. People instinctively root for the underdog. And they can't stand to see people treated unfairly—especially when they are not there to defend them-selves. Therefore, when discussing the business or individual with whom you are competing, remember this rule:

Never, never, never put down the competition.

Newspaper advertising is a highly competitive field, and in Southern California, the phrase "fiercely competitive" is quite appropriate. I discovered early in my career that unless I knew the competition as well as I knew my own product, my chances of success were slim. So I developed a series of strategies that have worked well over the years, and I would like to share them here.

Competitive Strategies—Always Fact, Never Fiction

A sales manager once called the sales manager for a compet-ing company to complain bitterly about the behavior of one of his men in the field. "He's going around telling people we're going out of business, and that's just not true!" yelled the first manager over the phone to his competitor. As he related this story to me later, the second manager, a close friend of mine, said he had all he could do to control his temper during this conversation. For the very thing he was complaining about was what several clients of my friend said he had done repeatedly in the past. Maintaining his temper, my friend assured the irate sales manager that he never would sanction such behavior, and that he would get to the bottom of it.

"The interesting thing about all of this," he recounted, "was that this irate gentleman was rumored to be doing the very thing he accused our company of. He lost several accounts right after this episode. I know our company said nothing about his going out of business, but it became apparent to all who did business with him during this time what he really thought of us, because the story of our alleged rumor spreading went with him on every business call he made."

What a shabby way to treat the competition—and a really stupid way to do business! You can never use fiction when talking about the competition (and rumors certainly qualify as fiction).

This sorry sales manager should have known better and would have done better if he had used one of these simple but effective selling strategies for dealing with the competition that involve fact, not fiction:

Know Your Competitor's Product. This is almost as valuable as knowing your own product. It is inconceivable to me that a Sharp Copier salesman not be conversant with all of the advantages of Xerox, IBM, Minolta, and any other competitive product that a potential customer might be considering. Or how about the car salesman, who almost always can find one of his models that is capable of going from zero to sixty miles per hour faster than the competitive car you told him you were thinking of buying. Consider the life insurance salesman, in a category almost as common as alligator shirts, yet having to somehow differentiate his business from all the other life insurance salesmen. And the way to differentiate, whatever you're selling, is to know your competition, just like you know your own product. Evaluate it from five key points of view: (1) product—what it is, what it does, etc.; (2) price—how much it is now, not what you thought you remembered it cost two years ago; (3) service—does it perform, does it have a good track record among other users; (4) results—does it more than meet the expectations of its customers; (5) cost efficiency—does it give real value for the money invested?

How Does Your Competition Compare With Your Product? When comparing what you are selling with your competition, you must be, or at least appear to be, as objective as you possibly can, for your potential client will be watching you for any signs of pettiness or unfairness. If the client asks, "How do you compare with the XYZ Company?" don't use the cliché "There is no comparison." You only insult his intelligence and classify yourself as either conceited or someone who doesn't know what he's talking about. Be positive, at all times, about your competitor, especially when showing how your product can do more for your client than your competitor's can. *Important:* If you know your competition is an issue with your client, you must bring it up. Don't be afraid, because the deadliest objection of all is the unstated objection. Say something such as, "I know you already buy from the XYZ Company, and what I would like to do is position my company alongside that company to see just how we compare in all areas of interest to your organization." With an approach like this, promising nothing but solid facts, your client will certainly want to know more, and will be greatly impressed as your knowledge of both companies is revealed point by point.

Use a Fact Comparison Sheet. One of the great newspapers of the United States is the *Los Angeles Times.* It is a fact and almost all intelligent individuals who work for any other newspaper would readily admit that. But at the same time, when the *Times* competes with a newspaper for advertisers—as it does with ours—it is mandatory that I know as many of the advantages there are to using our paper when compared with the *Los Angeles Times.* Consequently, for years I have used a fact sheet showing how the *Wave* compares with the *Times* in all significant areas of interest to advertisers. This fact sheet compares the two papers in all of the same categories, with the

Wave in one column and the *Times* in another. Although it may seem strange to someone not familiar with advertising, the *Wave* holds many clear-cut advantages over the behemoth *Times*. The fact sheet clearly spells those advantages out, and serves as a sales piece I can leave behind with the client. *Hint:* Add credibility by using facts directly from the source you are comparing. What better way to show competitive advantages to your product than to use your competitor's own material?

Always Be Fair. Companion advice for "Never run down the competition" is "Always be fair when comparing." Or, to put it another way, remember that many people believe the old saying "Figures don't lie, but liars figure." Don't fall prey to bending statistics to your own best interests. Basically, if you have to convolute a "fact" to where it would require three asterisks to properly explain all of the situations where it would not apply, then just don't use it. There is plenty of solid information available to make your case if you'll just look for it.

Remember this: The true spirit of competition is one of the cornerstones of success. If you are a professional salesperson, you have no guarantee of increased business—nor does your competition. But you had better always assume that the competition is working twenty-four hours a day to get ahead of you, and that it behooves you to be at least as knowledgeable in your field as the endless stream of competitors who have probably made calls on your prospect today.

Understand the nuance here. Competition shouldn't make you scared—it should make you sharp . . . alive and alert to the marketplace and its constantly changing environment. So keep up with the news, read trade journals, attend functions in your industry, and know your business. And while you're at it, study other companies' business, too. No matter how good it is, with the right approach and attitude, you'll find you can compete with the best of them.

Seven

Close in to a *Yes*

Each close you use should be an educational process by which you are able to raise the value of the product or service in the prospect's mind.

Zig Ziglar

Closing is the process of helping people make decisions that are good for them.

Tom Hopkins

I know a literary agent who was trying to wrap up a big book contract for his best author. He had three publishers very interested in the book, and was coming down to the last negotiating sessions with all of them. The first publisher—"A"—had international sales capabilities, and was offering the author what was, at that time, a huge cash advance. The second publisher—"B"—although quite a bit smaller, was offering almost the same amount of money as publisher A, and had the added advantage of more personalized service that often seems to go along with working with a small company.

The third publisher—"C"—was the firm that both the author and the agent wanted the most. For the kind of book the author was writing, and for that time in his career, this company afforded him not only a large sales organization and publishing prestige but also additional entrance to the widest possible market.

There was only one problem. Publisher C was not only far behind in the cash advance it was offering for the book but also the negotiating editor was sounding at best lukewarm on the project.

"It was a crisis in the negotiations," the literary agent recalled. "We really wanted publisher C to do the book, but we were bogged down in discussions that were going nowhere, and in great danger of losing the other two publishers. So I decided to concentrate on the competition, and dramatize just how badly the other firms wanted this book, something I really hadn't done before."

The turning point in closing the sale came during the course of one long telephone conversation with publisher C, when the agent said: "You know, Smith [not his real name] is a winning author. His last book was a best-seller, and he's known all over the world. He's put a lot of time and effort into this project, and your two competitors are both betting that it's going to be an even bigger seller than the first book. The book really belongs at your company, but unless the terms change, we're going to have to award this book to one of the other two companies."

Although the publisher was wavering, he wasn't quite sold

yet, according to the literary agent, who remembered with great glee the clincher—the final power close he used to summarize the competing companies' relative positions, and what could be gained with the right decision: "You know, this book contract is a little like a championship horse race, with potentially large financial reward to the winning publisher. The other two publishers have rounded the far turn and are heading for the finish line. And your company, which claims to know this project will be a real winner, hasn't even left the starting gate yet."

The points were summarized clearly, concisely, and with no beating around the bush. And that was exactly what it took. That was the turning point. With this very real challenge confronting him—to either bid aggressively for the book or risk losing it and a potentially large income to the competition—publisher C wasted no time in acting.

Within a day, the agent had the offer he wanted and his client went on to publish a very successful book that is selling well today. Everyone benefited because the agent had been willing to put everything on the line and challenge the publisher into realizing not only what he might stand to gain from the project but also what he stood to lose to his competition if he didn't take the book. The strategy worked for the following reasons:

1. *The salesman summarized both the advantages and the disadvantages of accepting or rejecting the project.*
2. *The salesman used an easily understood example—a horse race—to dramatize the relative positions of all the potential buyers of the book.*
3. *The salesman challenged his prospect to think seriously about what the loss of such a project might mean to his company—and what he stood to gain if he took it.*

A powerful close like this one in his selling of the book project wasn't something the agent consciously planned to do, but it is something that came about because he planned the basics of his presentation so well. He knew the value and potential value of what he was trying to sell. He knew everything he could possibly know about the three publishers who had expressed an interest in the project, and who ended up being the final bidders.

Especially valuable was the fact that he knew how fiercely competitive they all were, and he used that vital piece of information at just the right time. In short, he did his homework. Or, as I'm fond of telling my salespeople, "good inspiration comes from intense perspiration." For if you are ready, if you know all of the facts with regard to the needs of your potential customer and how you can fulfill those needs, then you have a real opportunity to be creative with a solid, powerful close at just the right time.

There's No Mystery in Closing

If you stop to think about it, there shouldn't be any great mystery to closing the sale. For closing the sale really means "making the sale," doesn't it? And isn't that what you are there to do in the first place? If you know the points well, you can summarize. A solid, 100 percent belief in your product, coupled with a small dose of courage, and you'll discover you have the ability to challenge. And if you really enjoy persuading someone to your point of view—thoroughly enjoy "being on stage," a quality that seems to be in abundance in all successful salespeople—you should have no problem dramatizing how successful the prospect will be if he or she buys what you are selling. (You may have to write down a few "dramatic analogies" until you really feel comfortable with this last point.

Caution: Dramatize sparingly, in selected situations where you really need to hammer home your point, or you feel the sale is drifting to nowhere. Otherwise, this type of close can seem out of place.)

That closing points can become easily lost in the give-and-take of a sales presentation—primarily the miscellaneous "other points" your prospect can bring up—is precisely why you need to focus and refocus on making your case clearly and concisely, to do your homework and know your product inside and out before you begin. When you are prepared, you know that you can close—and to help increase your sales chances, you'll remember this rule:

> *Dramatize . . . summarize . . . challenge—*
> *and turn the corner in closing and selling!*

Closing Begins With Product Knowledge and Enthusiasm

There are probably dozens—maybe hundreds—of specific closes that could be used for every possible sales situation, and many excellent books that analyze sales closes in detail. Reading books about closing can help to give you insights about what you should do to close a sale. You might even pick up an exact close or two you can use in your own profession. But in the long run, there is no substitute for product knowledge, and your own solid belief that you are helping someone who is definitely going to be better off because he bought your product or service.

Belief in what you are selling and a thorough product knowledge are the best one-two punch you can have when you are attempting to close a sale. With those two invaluable assets, you'll be able to attempt to close throughout your sales presentation, no matter how difficult the sales meeting, or how far off course you are led by your prospect.

And led off course you will be, as any veteran of sales meetings can attest. When that happens, and the subject turns to office politics, your prospect's summer vacation, the weather outside—or any number of topics other than your stated purpose—you must eventually bring the focus of the meeting back to why you came in the first place. And to do that, you must be able to hone in on the sales points you need to close the sale. As Zig Ziglar says it in his best-seller *Secrets of Closing the Sale:*

> Keep that issue focused. The story is told of a father in the Swiss Alps who sent his three sons out into the world. Before they made their departure he took them to a mountainside and instructed them to bring their crossbows. He said to the eldest one, "Aim your crossbow at the bird sitting on the ground some fifty feet away." The son did as instructed. The father asked the question, "What do you see?" The son replied, "I see the beautiful skyline, the gorgeous clouds, the majesty of God's universe." The father said, "That's good. Now, lower your bow."
>
> The second son was instructed to raise his crossbow and aim at the bird and he did. The father than asked the same question, "What do you see?" The second son said, "I see the beautiful mountains, the rolling valleys, the beautiful scenery with the rich grass." The father said, "That's good. Now lower your bow."
>
> The youngest son was then instructed to raise his bow and aim it at the bird, which he did. The father said, "What do you see?" The youngest son said, "I see where

the wings join the body," and with that he released the
arrow, which flew straight to the mark.

Point: When you're on a sales interview you have only
one target, which is to serve your customer by selling
your goods or services.[1]

Remember: In most cases, you called for the meeting. You
worked hard to get it, and presumably prepared just as hard for
it. So as your prospect responds to you, no matter how far
afield he may lead you, concentrate on why you are there.
Then at the first opportunity, without minimizing the prospect's conversation, bring him back to the points you had just
been making. Summarized, this rule can be stated this way:

Always keep your goal in sight—
and always work toward accomplishing it.

Read the Meeting as It Happens

Several years ago, I met the publisher of a small newspaper
who was intensely proud of his publication. Since it was a
small company he wore many hats, including selling much of
the advertising, the financial backbone of any community
paper. He related to me the story of how he finally was successful at gaining a large supermarket advertiser after months
of soliciting with no apparent interest.

"Even though the advertiser was questioning our newspaper's credibility because we were distributed free to the home
owners in our community, I kept coming back to how much I
personally could vouch for how well read the paper was because I had talked with so many people in the community
about the articles we were running, and had gotten so much

positive feedback from various organizations in our town. But no matter how much I talked in general terms, the advertiser was unconvinced, and I knew my precious interview time with him was slipping away. It became obvious that I needed to *show* this man rather than *tell* him that what I was saying was true. Suddenly I had a brainstorm, partly out of desperation but mostly out of the great faith I had in my newspaper and the firm conviction that we could really produce some advertising results for his company."

Pausing in reflection, he relished the moment all over again as he recounted how his challenge closed the sale with this particular advertiser. "I told him that we were convinced we could bring in more business for the stores he had in our area than he had ever seen before, and that we were prepared to back up our claim. I challenged him to run one ad, with especially low prices on selected items, just in our paper. If he would agree to do that, and pay us our regular ad price, I would help subsidize some of the losses he would take on the low-price items he was running just in our paper. Obviously, he would have to check his results to see how much we owed him, thus proving my point. But I still had some reservations as to how closely he would check the results, so I added one more element to the deal: a reader contest for a free television set, which I would pay for. Just fill out and mail in any one of several coupons you could find throughout my paper, and be eligible for the drawing, held the same week as the newspaper ad.

"He bought it, saying something like, 'If you have that much faith in your paper, the least I can do is buy one ad from you.' And while the results were good, the second part of the promotion—putting so much faith in all of the readers I said I had—was what really clinched the deal. He didn't buy my newspaper nearly as much as he bought my unswerving faith in my newspaper. Well, I was able to dump a cardboard box full of reader coupons (all trying for the free television set) on his desk, demonstrating once and for all that our paper was extremely well read. I believed it, and I was able to prove it beyond a shadow of a doubt to my first big advertiser, who went on to become a regular account in our paper."

Despite the objections, despite being led off track several times during the meeting, despite the cold responses, my publisher friend's faith in his particular product and his continual refocusing on the central issue of what the meeting was all about—that his little newspaper had enough readers to give continual, meaningful results to the advertiser—eventually led him to a creative sales close that proved beneficial for both him and his new client. The rule to be learned from this encounter is:

> *Know your product well enough to*
> *"create" a close on the spot.*

The Sales Close—Successful End to the Right Beginning

Ken Larson, Regional Director for Phoenix Mutual Insurance Company, is very emphatic about closing the sale. Perhaps it's because he has been so successful in sales throughout his career, having been honored as one of the top ten salespeople in his company twice while he was still a salesman. "The closing of the sale really begins with the opening of the sale," says Larson. "The better prepared the salesperson is at the start of the presentation, and the more he has prequalified his prospect's chances of buying what he is selling, the better off he is."

Preparation and prequalification. Those things you do early in the sales process are absolutely vital to its successful culmination. How well do you know your prospect and what he wants? Can you relate what he wants to your product or service—that is, will buying what you are selling help him get what he wants? Even more important, do you know what he doesn't like about your company? Can you bring up these arguments, which he may never do, and then dismiss them effectively? In other words, have you done a complete "prospect inventory" prior to going to your meeting? This principle of preparation and prequalification is the same whether you're selling pots and pans door-to-door, or are attempting to sell Congress on loan guarantees for your failing auto company.

By now, many of us are familiar with the legend of Lee Iacocca, the automotive genius who as Chairman of the Board for Chrysler Corporation took the number three automaker from the brink of oblivion and bankruptcy to a profitable, prosperous company in just four years. He was up against almost impossible odds in trying to get the government to guarantee huge loans while he worked at trimming the massive Chrysler inefficiency and developing the smaller, gas-saving cars America was buying in record numbers at that time. In his best-selling book, *Iacocca*, which chronicles this turbulent period from the late seventies to the early eighties, Lee Iacocca recalls how well prepared he was when he made his case by appealing to all the individual members of Congress on the very issues which held the most sensitivity: jobs and the economy. He writes:

> So we argued about competition and we argued about jobs. But most important of all were our arguments about economics . . . . The Treasury Department had estimated that if Chrysler collapsed, it would cost the country $2.7 billion during the first year alone in unemployment insurance and welfare payments due to all the layoffs. . . .

I said to the Congress: "You guys have a choice. Do you
want to pay the $2.7 billion now, or do you want to guar-
antee loans of half that amount with a good chance of
getting it all back? You can pay now or you can pay
later."

That's the kind of argument that causes people to sit up
and take notice. And it brings up an important lesson for
young people who may be reading this book—*always*
think in terms of the other person's interests.

In this case, I had to talk in terms of the representative
sitting in Congress. On ideological grounds, he might be
against helping us. But he sure changed his mind fast
after we did our homework and provided a district-by-
district breakdown of all the Chrysler-related jobs and
businesses in his state. When he realized how many people in his constituency depended upon Chrysler for their
living, it was farewell, ideology.[2]

Lee Iacocca was thoroughly prepared before he spoke one
word to Congress. He was prepared to do nothing else but succeed, which he did with a lot of hard work and his special
brand of persuasive, well-thought-out reasoning. He studied
every aspect of his argument, not only from his point of view
but also from the agenda of his prospect—in this case the
United States Congress. He did his homework, summarized
his argument beautifully, and while doing that, issued a dramatic challenge to his prospects in terms they would not only
have no problem understanding but could hardly refuse, based
upon how carefully and logically the facts were laid out. In
making this "sale," Iacocca illustrates another almost simplistic point about closing:

Closing the sale is the logical extension of a
well-planned and well-executed sales presentation.

That a sale has an excellent chance of being made given the
right execution of the "three Ps"—*prequalification, preparation,* and *presentation*—is not meant to demean, belittle, or
oversimplify selling and the selling process. On the contrary,
the exact opposite can be said about the successful close of the
sale.

Selling is not for fast talkers and slow walkers. Selling is
work—hard work, and lots of it. There can be some successful
closes with no work. I call that luck, and don't count on it to
eat regularly. There can be average success with an average
amount of work. I call that getting just what you worked for—
an average amount of success. Hopefully, you want more and
that is one of the reasons you are reading this book.

Then there is the salesman who succeeds more times than
he fails—the salesman who enjoys great success because he
knows what he must do each time he starts the selling process.
After the prospect analysis . . . after the preparation for the
meeting . . . after the arguments and the answers to the arguments . . . after the comeback from the bleakest possible situation—then and only then can he or anyone (including as
masterful a salesman as Lee Iacocca) hope to have continually
successful closes to any of his sales beginnings.

The Right Time to Close

There has been much said and written about this magic moment, and far more mystique than necessary attached to it.
The plain, unadorned truth of the matter is that you should
attempt to close your prospect from the first moment of con-

versation with him, and then regularly throughout the conversation thereafter.

Some people don't want to "offend" their prospects by being too forward too soon. Hogwash. Both you and your prospect know what you have in mind, so why put off the inevitable? Fear of rejection can be the only answer, so remember: *All he can do to you is say no.* What have you got to be afraid of? Your prospect can't read your mind, so go for it from the outset.

Obviously, from the first moment you need to attempt to close with manners, some common courtesy, and without excessively breathing down your prospect's back. But after observing standards of common human decency, drive straight for the sales close. You may be rewarded occasionally with a "no brainer"—that is, you might get a *yes* without having to work too hard for it. As one author put it, "One aggressive sales manager under whom I worked and learned gave me this tip: 'When you open your sales talk, drive straight for a close. Don't wander. Try to follow a step-by-step presentation for reaching your target, which is the sale of your product or service.' " [3]

The very first time you have a conversation with your prospect may be when you are agreeing on a time to meet to discuss what you are selling. Pursue the sale then, even if it's over the phone to someone you've never met. Say something like, "I think I have something you're really going to like. If after our meeting you agree, will you be in a position to make any kind of commitment for future business then?" This is an attempted partial close even before you have met with the prospect, so that even if he says no—the worst thing that could happen—you can usually get some kind of explanation about how he might ultimately be able to do business with you, and therefore have some extra, invaluable information you can put to your best advantage when you eventually go into the meeting.

Think about it this way: He hasn't met you yet, but he has agreed to see you. He hasn't had the opportunity to reject anything you are going to present, since you haven't presented it yet. You are only asking him a question about the mechanics of how he and his organization operate, and therefore not subjecting your presentation to the slightest risk. In fact, if you gain any kind of knowledge from this attempted presell at all, you are miles ahead in prequalifying your prospect. The rule on when to close can be summarized this way:

Attempt to close during your first conversation, and at selected times throughout your interview.

Closing During the Interview

The amount of information available on closing during the interview is absolutely awe-inspiring, as observed earlier in this chapter. Everyone who has used selling or persuasive techniques to make a living or in volunteer work has undoubtedly come across literature which promises to be "The Absolute, Ultimate, All You Need to Know Encyclopedia on Closing" in their quest to become more proficient in persuasion. Lecturers wax profoundly to rapt audiences on "surefire, can't-miss" closes; consultants meet with sales management groups to hear why their salesmen can't close and to offer costly suggestions. Then there are whole books dedicated to the subject, besides single chapters in many other books, as is the case here.

Let me say that much of this information is extremely beneficial, and worth the price of a book. There are some tremendous experts in the selling field who can teach salespeople at all levels something new in closing and how to close. But does it have to be made to seem so complex, confusing, and at times, overwhelming?

The answer is, of course not. I think it is mostly a case of our American "instant replay" mentality—that is to show us forty-seven different angles of the same play just because it's so important. There's no doubt about it—closing is important. It's vital—no, critical—to the success of the whole selling process. And while it is the heart and soul of the reason you are there in the first place—to get someone to buy what you are selling as quickly as possible—I would like to suggest that you demystify and simplify the closing process in your mind and realize that it is very basic and is something you can learn. In fact, everyone who has ever sold anything has had to learn how to close the sale. Very few people are born with this ability.

You too can become adept at closing the sale. When you have established a solid foundation of basic closing steps to take during an interview, you can then build on that foundation by applying those closing steps with greater skill in each successive interview. Here are a few basic steps I have found helpful throughout my career. Become familiar with these steps to closing success during the interview, and then apply them time after time and watch your sales climb.

1. *Ask for agreement from the outset.* Have you ever noticed that the people who seem to win arguments, whether in a business or social setting, are those people who ask lots of questions for which there can be nothing but agreement, or *yes* answers? These people have discovered that if they can get agreement on relatively minor points, they can slowly build a case of positive responses which ultimately will lead to the major *yes* on the major question. Politicians do this all the time when they weave flag, motherhood, and other nonargu-

able symbols into the fabric of their rhetoric. And of course, successful salespeople practice this same approach. They say things like, "I think you'll agree. We're both interested in more sales for your company," or "I'm here today to show you how our service can improve your company's position in the market. I think you and I are in agreement that that's a goal worth pursuing," or "The tax advantages to this plan are tremendous. You're interested in saving a few dollars on taxes, aren't you?" The idea here is to establish a rapport, to build a mountain of yeses which will make a no seem almost out of the question. Asking questions which can elicit only affirmative answers (or have at least a very high probability of getting yeses) is a vital way in the beginning of the interview of establishing your credibility and authority at the beginning of an interview. You avoid conflict (which in the beginning can be disastrous), the prospect gets a chance to know you and like you, and you are already a long way down the road to a successful close.

2. *Summarize the promise of the product often.* No matter how simple your message may be, it can seem extremely complex to the average listener, especially if he has been listening the way most people do. That is why internal summaries of what you have said up to various points must be given throughout your presentation. Again, as in the beginning, you should obtain agreement on the summarized points as much as possible. "Let me briefly summarize to make sure we're both on the same wavelength to this point," or "Are you with me on what I've outlined so far?" By gaining agreement an inch at a time, on parts of the presentation, you are slowly but surely gaining agreement on the entire presentation. And if there is disagreement or misunderstanding at some point along the way, you have given your prospect a chance to air that disagreement and dialogue with you about it. In this way, by the end of

the meeting, you should have cleared up all of the hidden objections and have a much better chance of closing your prospect. As one veteran sales and marketing executive said it:

> Hammer away on benefits to your prospect. Don't let up.
> Get your prospect to agree with you on those benefits.
> Each time you win his or her agreement, you are one step
> nearer to a smooth close and sale.[4]

3. *Use certain preplanned questions.* Along with obtaining
agreement from the outset and continually summarizing the
product benefits, the use of certain preplanned questions is another vital link in the chain of events leading to the successful
sales close. Before you ever set foot into the prospect's office,
you should know your planned interview well enough to know
when to ask these key questions. Any one of them asked at the
right time can make your sale. Asked at the wrong time, they
can seem out of place, and can set you back in your attempted
close. For example, if the prospect begins to talk about how
tight his budget is, what he is really doing is considering your
proposal and wrestling with how to fit it into his current
spending plan. Most companies or individuals never create
new money for what you are selling—instead, they must real-
locate existing money. Take advantage of this pondering to ask
a related question: "There are really two ways to go here, depending on your current budget—either a short test which will
cost very little, or a longer-term program which can be very
cost effective. Which do you think will work better for your
company?" Notice the positive way the salesperson engaged
the budget problem brought up by the prospect, ending in a
question whose answer could only benefit him. Other similar
types of questions are: "When do you normally like to take delivery? Of the three plans, which do you think best meets your

needs—A, B, or C? Would you rather buy in bulk, to get the discount, or in the smaller numbers we originally discussed?"

4. *At the end, if you don't close* ... No matter how well prepared or how well you execute your presentation and your attempted sales closes, there will often be times when the interview has come to an end and you haven't closed. Don't despair. A great many people simply need to think over the value of what they have heard and wouldn't have made a decision the first time around no matter how great the presentation. What is important here is remaining calm, confident, and in control of the situation. Don't ever show your disappointment. Stand up straight, give a firm handshake, and thank the prospect for his courtesy in listening to you. Then tell him of your intention to continue to pursue his business. Say something like, "I'll be calling you soon to let you know of any new developments which your company may be interested in. Is it better to call you the end of the week, or the beginning?" In this very positive way, no matter how disappointed or discouraged you may be, you are letting your prospect know that you really believe in what you are trying to persuade him to buy, and that you will be back to talk with him again at a time that is convenient. He will respect you for this graceful approach, and in the long run he may just buy what you are selling.

Determination—the Main Ingredient in Closing

If you've done everything I have suggested in this chapter and you don't see much improvement immediately, relax. Changing your approach takes time, especially when the mechanics of what you are attempting may be totally different. What is important is your commitment to change, your determination to be more successful in selling than you have been before. That is truly the monumental step, the biggest hurdle you had to overcome. Success will come gradually as you continue to work at your new skills and fine-tune them. Dr. Harold Blake Walker says:

> Don't be disappointed if you can't overhaul yourself from top to bottom overnight. There is more than a hint of warning in the comment of an illiterate farmer intent on learning to read and write. After some study, he took his pencil and began scribbling. Suddenly he shouted to his wife:"Maria, come here. I can write." She looked at his doodling and said: "Wonderful. What does it say?" "One thing at a time," he said, "I haven't learned how to read yet." [5]

Be Comfortable With Closing— It's Only Natural

In the end, after you have made a solid presentation, for which you were thoroughly prepared, to a well-qualified prospect, the chances are that you will close the sale. Why? Because that's why you are there in the first place. Maybe you'll close on the spot, maybe later. But know that you will close. And while you're at it, be happy and excited about closing. For you're really trying to help someone do something you feel is in his best interests, but which he is resisting because making a decision to do anything new is a painful process to most people.

That you are there with great and genuine enthusiasm as the persuader to help him do this because it will benefit him should make you feel proud about your efforts. Or, as my friend Ken Larson puts it, "They have just purchased to your need, and you've just sold to theirs."

That's a win-win situation, isn't it? And that's what successful closing—and selling—should always be. If both parties benefit, it will always work. If only one party benefits, it will hardly ever work. The important thing is to be comfortable with the close. Know that when you have put the other person's agenda ahead of your own, that you have a product, service, or idea that is truly going to benefit him, asking for the order is as natural as breathing. And in selling, there is no breathing without closing.

Eight

Coming Back
From a *No*

If you are thinking thoughts of defeat, I urge
you to rid yourself of such thoughts, for as
you think defeat you tend to get it.

Norman Vincent Peale

It had taken the insurance executive weeks to get an appointment with his elusive prospective customer, a good client who the salesman was convinced needed more insurance. The meeting was for lunch, and as the salesman waited in the reception area for his client, he went over all the ways he could bring up the idea of more insurance in the most natural way possible. After all, the man had been a tough sell to begin with, was an acknowledged frugal businessman, and almost always

121

seemed to resent the idea of business being discussed over lunch or during any other social occasion.

Suddenly the door to the reception area burst open and through it strode the customer, who while extending his hand in the general direction of the salesman, blurted out, "How are you, George? Listen, I'll go to lunch with you, but I only have an hour. Things have been really hectic here, and I need to get back soon. Oh, and something else. The last thing I want to do is buy more insurance."

As soon as the last phrase was out of the customer's mouth, my insurance friend smiled. For even though it was brought up in a negative way, the client himself had solved George's problem. Insurance was obviously on his mind because he said, "I don't want to talk about it." So why was George smiling to himself? Because he knew he could discuss the subject of insurance during the lunch hour, since it was on the client's mind. There was something the client wanted to talk about since he had brought the subject up, and even though there was a solid *no* before the first words of George's sales presentation could be uttered, George knew he had a good chance for making solid arguments for the additional insurance.

"That first *no*, before we even shook hands, was the turning point in that particular sale," chuckled George, recalling the sale with great fondness, "for he had given me a clearly stated objection—that he was against more insurance—before I brought up the subject myself. He wanted to talk about it in spite of what he actually said, and he gave me the ammunition necessary to go to work, which I did throughout lunch. The fact that we spent almost two hours together instead of the hour he said he had indicates how interested he was in the topic of insurance. But the real indicator was the extra sale I made that day, in spite of what he had told me just before our meeting."

To summarize what George knew when he heard that first, definite *no*:

> **Learn to recognize when no does not mean no,**
> **but is a request for more information.**

For George, the turning point in that sale came with the customer's very emphatic no. From that point, through probing and asking what he felt about his current policy, George found out the real reason for the negative comment. Although the client was thinking about buying more insurance, his wife had told him how much she hated insurance, couldn't see its value, and thought it was just a big drain on their cash. She was the bookkeeper in the family and hated to write what she thought was a huge check every month for nothing. Hence, the customer's strong position to George.

"Over the course of that lunch," he explained, "we worked out a better plan that was financially easier for them to handle, and at the same time was building cash value for their retirement. I also made an appointment to explain it to both him and his wife, so that all of the decision makers would be in on the presentation at the same time."

The real lesson here is that *no* does not have to be the end. In fact, it is often the beginning, echoing the famous title from the successful sales book by Elmer G. Letterman: *The Sale Begins When the Customer Says No.*

If at All Possible, Agree With the Stated Objection

A *Wave* salesman once came to me enormously frustrated because he had not been able to convince the manager of a large department store to advertise in our paper. "He agrees we have a good paper, he agrees we reach his customers and would probably get him good results, but then he says he just can't afford any more advertising, no matter how good. I argue and argue with him, pointing out that if he likes our paper he should give us a try. But he stubbornly tells me he just can't afford it. I don't know what else to do."

Although I wasn't sure what more I could add, I said I would go with the salesman on his next call to the potential customer. We made an appointment for lunch with him in the coffee shop of his store, and it was there that I saw exactly what was going wrong with this potential sale. After my salesman had completed his presentation, which was very strong, the store manager accepted most of the points and then came back with the same basic objection he had always made—that he couldn't afford any more advertising, no matter how good it was.

As my salesman started to argue, just as he always had with this prospective account, I interrupted. "Excuse me," I said. "Although I don't know your company as well as Jim does, I can certainly see the validity of what you're saying. Advertising to you, although valuable, is another expense, and the more advertising you add, the less your profit. So what you're really saying is that you're spending enough money right now on this area of your business, and to spend any more would be to cut further into your profit."

The store manager stopped right in his tracks. "Yes," he said. "That's exactly right. You see the point very clearly. I'd like to use your paper, but I just can't afford to with all the money I'm spending in other advertising right now."

"Listen, I don't want to add to your problems," I said. "I'm really here to help eliminate some of them. And if I were you, I wouldn't spend any more money in advertising, either. What I would like to propose is reallocating some of your current expenditures, and I think I can show you a way to get greater results than you're currently achieving and at a lower cost."

Let me tell you this man literally jumped at the chance to hear what I had in mind, which was really very simple: taking a percentage of the money he was currently spending and testing the papers he was using and ours over a period of eight weeks, with smaller but equal-sized ads for both papers. At the end of that time, he could decide what paper or papers had brought in the best results, and intensify that schedule while dropping the media that didn't work, thereby increasing his results in a more cost-effective advertising medium—exactly what I said would happen.

The reason I was successful and my salesman was not became apparent to me once I was in the meeting. The fact was that my salesman was arguing tooth and nail with the customer over something he already had agreed with—that our newspaper was a worthwhile place to put his advertising. He wasn't shedding any additional light on the prospect's complaint, and by arguing was further entrenching the prospect in his definite *no* posture. What the real issue was, and the objection the salesman wasn't even answering, was the whole problem of the man's budget. It was already spent, and he didn't know of a way to use our paper without spending more money, which he clearly didn't want to do. What he wanted but wasn't saying in so many words was a suggestion from us as to how he could best spend his current advertising budget, not our continual harangue to increase it. By seeing this point, and agreeing with him, we were finally able to get around his no-money argument with a solid plan that not only showed the value of our paper, but also gave us a continuing account and allowed him to lower his ad budget. The moral of the story?

Know when to give in, a retreat that
should be only temporary.

Remember—an objection means dialogue. And dialogue means you've got a great chance to be successful, because you're the salesman with complete knowledge of your clients' needs and how your product or service can help to solve those needs. Don't run from an objection. Be happy you've got one, because it gives you a chance to do your thing. Confront it eagerly, happily, with a phrase such as, "I'm glad you brought that up" or, "I'm certainly glad to hear what you have to say. I can really see what you're talking about, and it makes a lot of sense." All of this leads easily to a related rule, which appears to be rooted in common sense, but which for some reason or other is often ignored by salespeople who have more desire to defend their egos than to make the sale. Simply stated it is this:

Avoid direct confrontation when you hear "no"—
use the "I agree, but . . ." approach.

Whatever the phrase, once you start agreeing with someone, you change the dynamics of the situation. You are now on his side, not on the opposing side. "I really see what you mean. You have quite a problem," or "You know, I never looked at it quite that way before," or "You're absolutely right! These are difficult times, and budgets are tight. I've heard that same thing from several people who have become customers of mine just recently." Whatever the case, if you can take a fall-back position without compromising yourself or what you are selling, it will be well worth it to give validity to and acknowledge the other person's point of view.

Treat Your Prospect Like a Close Friend

Think of the client objection as part of a conversation you are having with a close and respected friend. You will undoubtedly think very carefully over everything this friend says, even though you may disagree, before making your point. After all, you have a friendship to consider, and that's what friends do. They give credence and respect to each other's opinion, while still hanging on to their own ideas. Shouldn't you be treating your prospect and potential client/friend the same way? Their stated objections certainly have some validity to them, so do all you can to see their point of view, acknowledge it in some way, and then ease into the point you want to make. If you have been particularly argumentative with your clients in the past, and have gotten nowhere for it, try this "Yes, but . . ." approach. Saying "I agree with you" is music to most people's ears, and with two people in agreement on one major issue, other agreement must surely follow, tremendously enhancing your chances for agreement on the major issue—whether or not the prospect will buy what you are selling.

The late Dale Carnegie summed up the power of this kind of thinking in his legendary best-seller, *How to Win Friends and Influence People.* Carnegie was recalling how a man in one of his classes had a selling style that was extremely confrontational. He was a dismal failure in the business of selling trucks because as soon as anyone brought up anything negative about the trucks he was selling, boom!—he attacked and really let him have it for criticizing his product. Carnegie recalls his approach to this difficult student:

> My first problem was not to teach Patrick J. O'Haire to talk. My immediate task was to train him to refrain from

talking and to avoid verbal fights. Mr. O'Haire became one of the star salesmen for the White Motor Company in New York. How did he do it? Here is his story in his own words: "If I walk into a buyer's office now and he says: 'What? A White truck? They're no good! I wouldn't take one if you gave it to me. I'm going to buy the Whose-It truck,' I say, 'The Whose-It is a good truck. If you buy the Whose-It, you'll never make a mistake. The Whose-Its are made by a fine company and sold by good people.'

"He is speechless then. There is no room for an argument. If he says the Whose-It is best and I say sure it is, he has to stop. He can't keep on all afternoon saying, 'It's the best' when I'm agreeing with him. We then get off the subject of Whose-It and I begin to talk about the good points of the White truck."[1]

The lesson here is easy to see: When you are selling or persuading and the objection looks like a stone wall, don't keep butting your head against it. It's not only very painful but you also really don't get anywhere. Instead, see the other side, and give the prospect the respect for his opinions you would grant to a close friend. Recognize the merit of the other person's opinion. There is great value in this selfless "others agenda" approach that may be just the key you need to turn the corner in your selling, and establish a solid, long-term relationship at the same time.

Taking a *No* in Stride

What is your reaction when you hear the word *no*? Disappointment? That's natural. Depression? A certain amount. Fatalism? In other words, you had this interview all figured out, and you expected as much. In fact, you might have been surprised if you had succeeded.

While all of the above emotions can be classified as normal reactions to a *no* or a string of *nos*, they can also be classified as The Loser's Creed if they last for more than a brief time. For the salesman to be really effective, to be more than just a paid conversationalist, he must feel one more emotion to be truly effective after a turndown. He must feel determination. Use determination to analyze why it happened. Where did the presentation go wrong? What must you do to make the next one right? To the successful salesman, a *no* is like another clue to a detective . . . an additional piece of evidence for him to think about, solve if possible, and thus move closer to a successful sales close. If he has successfully prequalified his prospect, if he knows that prospect should buy what he is selling, and if he is determined, the *no* is merely one more step he has to take to reach the inevitability of *yes*, the answer he started out to get and for which *no* is not an acceptable substitute.

Therefore, a *no* can really be looked at in a positive sense. As Richard Buskirk says:

> Prospects who voice honest objections are assisting you by telling you how far away you are from a sale. They are also providing more valuable information about what it will take to make the sale than all the preapproach data you have assembled.[2]

So welcome the *no*, but at the same time be determined to take it apart in sections, to analyze everything about why it occurred so you can come back with answers that will overcome it. Obviously, if you can derail the *no* right on the spot, then you are much better off. But if not, leave yourself room to come back and fight another day. Say something such as, "I really appreciate your time, and I respect your decision, although I obviously can't agree with it. I would love the opportunity of carefully considering everything you have said, and then exploring with you at some future date how to surmount these problems and meet your needs in some alternative ways," or simply, "When can I call you?" This rule can be summarized this way:

Take the no gracefully—
and lay the groundwork for coming back.

The Anatomy of a *No*: Strategies for Coming Back

Ken Larson is Regional Director for Phoenix Mutual, one of the largest life and health insurance companies in America. As one of the top salespeople in his company, and as one of its primary field management figures directing dozens of salespeople, Larson has risen to the top of his field, in large part because of tenacity and perseverance—his determination to come back and sell resistant accounts in one of our country's most highly competitive occupations. In a recent discussion, I asked him what he did to come back from a *no* after he thought he had done everything he possibly could.

"To begin with, I try to stay calm," he said. "Then, if I don't happen to be in the office with the prospect at the time, I will either arrange another meeting or call him on the telephone for the sole reason of finding out why. I then probe, asking every conceivable question regarding why the presentation went sour—wrong timing, wrong person, budget problems, etc. Finally, after I am fairly certain why the presentation was rejected, I ask the prospect what it will take to get a *yes*. There are no vague reasons or 'I don't knows' they can give me, because I have already found out from them why we got a no instead of a yes. I am now in a position to say, 'Well, if I'm able to solve this particular problem you just brought up, I should be able to get a yes.' Only by probing first can I put myself in this advantageous position of finding out exactly what objection I must eliminate before I can make the sale. Then the rest is a matter of doing what I'm paid to do."

Probing for the Problem

It is no wonder that Ken Larson has achieved great success in his company and his industry. He has developed an automatic response to a *no*—determination to find out the reason for the turndown, and then an equal amount of resolve to ask the client for the order once again, based upon the information he had found out from his extensive probe. Let's examine some of the questions Larson and other successful salespeople might ask after receiving a *no*:

Possibility #1: Wrong Person. Did you see the decision maker? Is there a committee in on the decision? Ask how the decision-making process works, and you should be able to find out if you somehow got directed to the wrong office. Egos have a lot to do with this problem. As incredible as it may seem, you may not ever be told that you were in the wrong office, but may have to find out through company organizational charts, directories, anonymous calls into the company switchboard to ask job responsibilities. If you can't get to the decision maker, then find out who has recommending power. Remember: *You can't make the sale if you don't get an offer presented in the right office.*

Possibility #2: Wrong Time. Your timing may be off because new offers aren't even being considered by your prospect.

For example, the company has just been sold, so there are new executives you'll have to see later. Whatever the reason, if your timing isn't right, your chances of making the sale are greatly diminished.

Possibility #3: Budget Problem. If all the money has been allocated for your type of product or service, you need to know that so you can make some alternative suggestions to the prospect.

Possibility #4: The Program. Ask the prospect, "What did you think of my program? Was there some specific part about it you didn't like?" Getting him into a dialogue on specific parts of the program may isolate exactly where it went wrong.

Possibility #5: You and the Presentation. As painful as it may be, you must find out how you did. Ask the prospect, "Was there a problem with me, or the way I presented the material?" Or, "Did I present everything clearly? Did you understand the primary advantage?" (Then name your strongest advantage.) If there was something you didn't do, you may not get the order this time, but armed with this new information, your presentation should be greatly improved next time.

Possibility #6: Your Company. There may be a negative perception of your company which never came out in the meeting but which is blocking the sale. Perhaps your competition has been planting some negative seeds. Or maybe your prospect perceives your company to be much smaller than it is, with far fewer capabilities to deliver the product. No matter that the prospect's unstated negative perception of your company may be dead wrong, it is part of the prospect's reality and is therefore 100 percent right until you discover that this feeling exists and then proceed to successfully discount it to the prospect.

When there is a *no*, there are usually good reasons for it, just as there are always good, solid reasons for making your points and persuading your prospect. In the case of a *no*, the salesman should never consider himself defenseless. On the contrary, if he learns to develop the patience of a good detective, the empathy of one who can see what the prospect sees and has no axe to grind, and the skill of a surgeon in probing for the problem, he will find why his proposal was rejected, and then at least have a chance to come back. It is a process that takes time and energy, but it can be well worth it in the long run.

When All Else Fails, Keep the *No* in Perspective

During an average week, if I get plenty of sleep, don't get any unexpected bills, keep my fried foods to a minimum, and manage to ignore the incessant ring of my daughter's telephone (strange how the bills for her calls keep coming to us), I can generally put this selling career I have chosen for my life's work into proper perspective. No matter how many rejections I may have endured, no matter how many solid *no* answers I have received to my sales question, I am sure of one thing: God has truly blessed me with a wonderful family, a happy and successful marriage, a home, vacations, and all the amenities that go with a modicum of success in my business. So that when I have a bad week, have just lost two accounts, been turned down by two others I thought I would get, and had three consecutive important meetings canceled, I eventually get back to reflecting on what this selling career has given me—and that is a tremendously rewarding life in an occupation I genuinely enjoy.

Oh, sure, after I've been rejected I get depressed, just like anyone else. I get angry, just like anyone else. And at times, I will even develop a martyr complex (you know, the "why me" question, asked over and over again). But fortunately, none of this ever lasts very long. Usually, after my anger and disappointment subside, and I am able to reflect on it, I offer a silent private moment of prayer. It is then that an enormous feeling of relief sweeps over me as I realize how truly fortunate I am to actually be doing something I like and getting paid for it besides. After all, it is only some minor defeat, some temporary rejection, and in the greater scheme of things, truly trivial. Shortly after that, depression and anger give way to determination, all my old confidence returns, and I'm back on the job, trying to figure out how to overturn those rejections and get them onto my scoreboard.

I am especially helped during times like this when I hear of someone with great courage, who in a life-threatening situation has come back against incredible odds. Ted Campbell is such a person. A gifted football player for Azusa Pacific College, Campbell's seemingly fit, healthy body was stricken with cancer during the height of his college career. According to the *Los Angeles Times*, in a story entitled "Campbell Runs Life's Ultimate Comeback Route," Ted Campbell is a fighter who refused to take the ultimate *no* for an answer:

> Campbell, 23, is playing football again, and playing it well for Azusa Pacific after undergoing major cancer surgery twice and extensive chemotherapy treatments during the last two years.
>
> It has been a long and difficult fight for the 6-foot, 180-pound senior, whose weight dropped to 139 pounds during his ordeal.

But at no time did Campbell doubt he would play football again. "Every opponent I've ever gone up against, I thought I could beat," Campbell said. "I thought I could overcome [cancer]. It was like I was preparing for a football game and this was the toughest opponent I'd ever faced." [3]

Campbell won his battle primarily because of his attitude. He didn't feel sorry for himself for any extended length of time. He didn't accept his fate. On the contrary, he was determined to beat the cancer and return to a normal life. Even after a relapse almost took his life, "Campbell . . . never lost his will to live. 'There are only two ways you can look at it,' he said. 'You can get mad at God and say, "Why did You do this to me?" or you can say you're going to fight it.' " [4]

Have you had many comebacks lately? If not, maybe it's because you just haven't tried. And why not? After all, nothing from nothing is nothing. So square your shoulders, plant your feet, grit your teeth, and get back in the game. It's a great game, and you've really got nothing to lose. In fact, you just might have a great deal to gain. Ask Ted Campbell:

It was an ecstatic moment when Campbell scored his first touchdown on a 66-yard pass play in the first quarter of a game against Claremont-Mudd Sept. 21.

"When I scored that touchdown, I held the ball up and said, 'God this is for you.' " [5]

PART III

A LITTLE MORE EFFORT
CAN MEAN
A LOT MORE SUCCESS

Nine

Build a Bridge
Between Interviews

Speech is civilization itself. The word, even the most contradictory word, preserves contact—it is silence which isolates.

Thomas Mann

. . . simple, direct writing is a valuable tool for salesmen to have and use. You'll want to make your letters, reports, and memos your faithful ambassadors. When you let them represent you and your company as they should, you're the winner.

James F. Bender

One of the most popular recent television commercials for a phone company shows a wonderful old couple who obviously have just been talking to their son on the telephone. When the husband asks his wife why she's crying, she says simply, "Because he said, 'I love you, Mom.' " Shortly after that, the commercial's theme, "Reach Out and Touch Someone" is played and as the advertisement comes to an end, "warm fuzzies" well up in millions of people around the country who have just experienced a special personal touch (albeit thirdhand and by way of the tube).

What is the reason for the success of this and a series of other "Reach Out and Touch Someone" TV and radio commercials? Straightforward, warm communications that convey genuine caring are the most highly valued kinds of communications we enjoy today. And unfortunately, among the least experienced. Mechanization, computerization, high-speed transportation—many of the modern conveniences we hold most dear—have made us more efficient, but have left us little time to be real people who convey real feelings verbally and in writing to those with whom we are close as well as to those with whom we do business. A premium is placed on speed, efficiency, and production—not warmth, caring, and concern. Yes, we have TV, radio, telephones, car telephones, computers, newspapers, billboards, skywriting, etc., etc. We are the most communication-oriented society of all time, yet less personal communication gets accomplished than ever before in history.

The tragedy of divorce, and situations in which people who live in the same house often don't speak, are sad examples of our lack of personal communication. Another example is your cluttered mailbox. You can tell just how little value is placed on personal communication by the machine-generated letters and brochures that are sent out every day. (The "personal urgent-o-gram" I received just the other day was for a land pro-

motion that was about as urgent as the threat of seven-year lo-
custs in the Los Angeles suburb where I live.)

How does all of this apply to selling, and turning the corner
in your own personal selling efforts? Well, I maintain that after
the interview—after this important meeting you've spent valuable time to arrange, prepare for, and conduct—you simply
don't walk away from the meeting without thinking about
communicating. Again. And again. And again. And with some
sort of personal touch. After all, you wouldn't have taken the
time to have a meeting in the first place if your prospect wasn't
qualified to benefit from what you sell. So why not attempt to
cement the relationship with some solid, effective communication after the interview?

Initiate Personal Contact

We're not talking about making sure your prospect gets a
copy of the company newsletter. Or that you follow up with
the company's latest computer sales letter, complete with the
prospect's name inserted several times in the text so that it
looks as though it were typed just for him. You probably want
to make sure that he receives those, too. But if he receives this
nonpersonal, mass-market type of approach *in place of* your
own personal communication—that special signature that says
without a doubt, you took the time to communicate—then
you are missing the point. In fact, it is a point so worth making
that I want to interrupt this section to emphasize it as follows:

*There can never be too much personal communication
between interviews.*

The second line of a popular song really says it best: "I just
called to say how much I care." Whether you're calling or

writing after the interview, this special action that you initiate should show care, a concern for the other person's agenda, and gratitude for the time he or she spent to talk to you. Almost everyone knows how valuable time in any block of seconds, minutes, or hours is today. It is so valuable that your prospect will immediately recognize the time and trouble you took to personally let him know you were thinking of him.

Brief Notes Can Mean Long Relationships

Are you doing all the writing you should in your sales work? Or, is your writing suffering, or even nonexistent, because you rationalize that you just don't have the talent or the time for that kind of thing—that all of your persuading is done verbally anyway, and that writing is just a waste of time? Whatever the reason, if you are not writing at least a brief note after each interview, you're missing a chance to sell more of your product or service. If you don't believe it, consider these solid reasons for following up in writing. I call them *written bridge builders* (reasons to write):

1. *To sell your product when you can't be there.* Obviously, your prospect isn't going to let you live at his office all day. So on the days you don't see or talk to him, your letter can serve as your salesman—an additional silent sales tool can be as effective as your own presentation, in summing up company advantages, why the prospect should buy now, and other precise reasons you have had a chance to reflect on after your meeting.

2. *To establish the relationship.* A letter can give your prospect the impression that you are a thoughtful salesperson—you care about his business, so much so that you took the time to write. And although it's not always immediately obvious,

your prospect will give you new respect for taking the time to correspond.

3. *To provide requested information.* All questions that a prospect has can't always be answered in the course of the sales presentation. And as busy as most people are, getting the prospect on the phone to clear up those unanswered questions often proves impossible, let alone impractical. That's when a short, follow-up letter giving the prospect information he has actually requested can be an extremely potent sales tool.

4. *To thank the prospect for his time.* This is perhaps the single most important use of the business follow-up letter, and certainly one of the least-thought-of reasons for writing. But just think of the power contained in the words thank you. If that were all you said in your follow-up letter, you would be on your way to becoming a most successful "communications bridge builder." (More about the power of "thank you" in chapter 11.)

I know of a young salesman who is successful today because he practiced a combination of written and verbal "bridge building" techniques. He worked for another publication and had just persuaded a large, potentially lucrative retailer to advertise in his newspaper. There was only one problem: by the time the retailer was able to get the advertising ready, it almost always seemed to be past his paper's deadline.

"Boy, was I frustrated," he recalled to me later. "I had told my boss I had the account, I *knew* I had the account, and the advertising manager wanted to give me all of his advertising. But I actually ended up getting very little of it in those first weeks."

He went on to say how the advertising manager said that his staff, which had been cut recently, was being pushed to the limit. The addition of my friend's paper seemed like extra work to them, so they always did his ad last, which almost always resulted in the ad's being left out.

"I was getting one ad out of eight that I should have been receiving," he recalled. "I developed a big credibility gap with my boss, who was really on my case about the ads that should have come in, but didn't. I didn't know what to do, and the ad manager appeared to have his hands tied. So in desperation, I called the account and found out the names of the advertising artists who put my ad together, even though I normally would have no reason to ever talk to them. I then resolved to send both of them a short note every week, taking care to avoid expressing my frustration, accentuating the positive instead, hoping to find some way to help them resolve their problem of getting our ads produced so late.

"Week number one, my letter read:

> Just a brief note to say thanks for working on my ad. I know how busy you are, and I just wanted you to know how grateful we are for your business, and for the extra effort you are having to make to produce our advertising. Let me know if there is anything I can do to help you.

"Two days later, I got a call from one of the artists, who was pretty indignant—hardly the response I had expected. He wanted to know why we had such an early deadline, that it was really pushing them beyond their limits, and that they didn't know if they could ever get our advertising out with the small staff and short amount of time they had to work on it. As best I could, I tried to help them with detailed information about our paper's production needs, and then extended our deadline to its very limit, something we did for very few customers. (I had explained all of this to the advertising manager, but it sounded as though he had never passed it on to his irritable and overworked staff.) The artist thanked me curtly for the new information, and said he would do his best.

"I immediately sent out a second note, which briefly thanked him for his time, reiterated much of what I had told him about deadlines, and once again pledged to do anything I could do to help make his job easier with respect to our publication. The upshot of the whole thing was that they made the next week's deadline (barely, but they made it) and from that point on made about 90 percent of the issues they were scheduled to go in—and all because of some brief written and then verbal follow-up communication, which emphasized how much I appreciated their work and added a sincere offer to help them as much as possible to make our deadline."

My friend was really a bridge builder in the best sense, using letters and then the telephone to build a solid bridge of communications between himself and the client to salvage the advertising schedule he had worked so hard to sell.

The value of mastering post-interview bridge building cannot be overstated. Even something as seemingly unimportant as a brief "thank you" is perceived by the best and most successful salespeople as one of their most powerful communications bridge builders. A salesman I know keeps Hallmark in business with the bundles of thank-you notes he buys. He carries around a pocketful of them just to make sure he sends out several brief thank-you notes during each of his busy weeks.

Whether it is to thank people, to straighten out a problem that is holding up a big sale, to lay out the details of a new sales proposal, to supply requested information—or any one of a dozen other reasons—use the sales letter to help you turn the corner in your selling. Think of it as an extra salesman working for you, your personal handwritten ambassador carrying your most powerful sales arguments, your best wishes, and your own unique personality past the waiting-room doors, past the secretary, and into the hands of your prospect, after which you can greatly increase your chances for making the sale.

Got Hang-ups About Phone Follow-up?

If familiarity breeds contempt, too many follow-up phone calls from a salesman in a short period of time can breed absolute disgust, followed by the old "He's out of the country" excuse every time the salesman phones thereafter. But for the salesman who uses selectivity in his phone follow-up, it doesn't have to be—nor should it be—that way.

I personally prefer the phone follow-up method to the written follow-up method (hardly a headline to my long-suffering relatives, who have received far more phone calls than letters from me), although both methods have their time and place and should be used together on every prospect.

Not all salespeople feel the way I do, however, and some are greatly intimidated by the telephone. That the phone can be one of the great sales tools is indisputable and has been taken up in some detail in chapter 4, "Telemarketing—Direct Line to More Sales." The balance of this chapter will deal with how the phone should be used effectively in sales follow-up, and will show how it can be coordinated with written follow-up for a maximum sales effort.

Avoid the "Columbo" Approach

Several years ago the fine actor Peter Falk made famous the disheveled and supposedly bumbling detective Columbo in the television series of the same name. Columbo's technique was to interrupt his prime murder suspect as many times as possible, both in person and on the phone. He would phone several times during the day. He would call unannounced at the suspect's home or office, and would always start out the conversation with, "I really hate to bother you, but . . . " or, "I know I'm probably makin' a pest of myself, but . . . " True to television, Columbo always got his man through his offensive, badgering technique, which could be called relentless, brilliant detective work.

Although a master of strategy and deduction (good qualities for detectives *and* salesmen), as a salesman, Columbo would have been a flop. The fact is there are many Columbo types in selling who, although filled with all sorts of knowledge, oppressively foist themselves on their poor prospects and then wonder why they can't make the sale, regardless of how sound their logic or advantageous their sales arguments.

I have just completed an excruciating ordeal called "buying a car." If part of the American Dream is owning your own car(s), then shopping for one can surely be dubbed the American Nightmare. I went from dealer to dealer, all of whom insisted they had the right car at the right price for me. And none of the offers were exactly comparable. They each varied their deal just enough—with equipment options, financing, length of time to pay back the loan—so that there was no way I could compare apples with apples. In the five dealerships I shopped, I had five different kinds of prices and deals.

Thoroughly annoyed with the whole process and no closer to making a decision than when I started, I received a phone call from the sales manager of the dealership I had gone to first, because they were advertising both the best price and the best terms.

The manager's name was Ed, and he wanted to know when I was going to pick up my car. Poor Ed. Because he reached me at the height of my frustration, I vented my spleen on how little I thought of his salesman—that he was following up with me just fine, but was not giving me the exact competitive in-

formation I needed to make a decision. Furthermore, the salesman told me he couldn't get my color, that I had better buy
now while the sale was still in progress, and that I should settle
for my second or third choice in color combination. In fact, I
said, he was trying to push me into making a decision to buy a
car I really didn't want without the information I needed. He
was in effect pushing me right out of doing business with his
company and into a competing dealership.

Right after that, I got action. Ed gave me the numbers I
needed, I received the service I thought I should have been
getting all along, and his follow-up telephone calls were intelligent, thoughtful, and totally considerate of my needs—not the
persistent, unproductive calls made by his salesman. Well, I
bought my car from Ed after all, and the only really unfortu-
nate thing about the whole experience was that I had to get
angry to get action. Salesmen sell to very few angry prospects.

But Ed won a customer with his thoroughly professional
treatment of me, and unless I miss my guess, I think he also
straightened out my original hardworking but misguided salesman, who had faithfully followed up with me and told me
everything about the car I was thinking of buying except what
I wanted to know.

Don't misunderstand—I'm not contradicting my earlier
point that there can never be too much personal communication between interviews. That statement is absolutely true. But
it's also true that this important follow-up communication
must be planned and coordinated so that the prospect isn't
pressured and harassed in the process.

To avoid the Columbo approach to telephoning (remember—the suspect had to listen because he was guilty; your prospect can hang up on you at any time), and since a phone is so
much greater an intruder than a letter, here are some tele-

phone follow-up "do's" and "don'ts" which can help to make you a more effective verbal bridge builder:

Do:

Call within one week after your initial meeting.

Call when the prospect asked you to call.

Call whenever you have new, valuable information not originally given to the prospect.

Call to relate to the prospect's personal life (within bounds, of course—birthday, promotion, etc.).

Call to invite the prospect to business lunch. (Make sure to have something to talk about.)

Call when you've done everything expected of you, and you feel you're not getting anywhere. (Say, "I'm really puzzled. I feel as though there's some question I haven't answered.")

Call when you know you've received all the business you can get from that particular client. (Say, "I think I've sold you just about everything I can. I just called to see if there's anything more I can do for you, get you out to a relaxing lunch," etc.)

Call to say thanks for his or her time, consideration, business, or whatever is appropriate.

Don't:

Call to reconfirm an appointment, unless asked to by the prospect. A phone call only gives the prospect a chance to cancel or postpone your important interview. (Always confirm your interviews in writing—then the burden is on your prospect to call or write to cancel.)

Call so often that you rush the prospect into a negative decision—that is, he decides not to buy because he hasn't had the time to look at your proposal, and he feels bad about holding you up. (Why does he feel bad? Because you keep pestering him for a decision without giving him any new information.)

Call without a precise plan of what you are going to say. (Or, don't waste your prospect's valuable time.)
Call twice in the same day. (If you appear anxious, your prospect will almost surely assume you are unsure of yourself and project that uncertainty to whatever it is you're trying to sell him.)

Meeting, Writing, Phoning—
a Coordinated Effort

The essence of good follow-up is to coordinate it all—to orchestrate it with your original meeting. The sale is your symphony, and you are the conductor. Your particular composition, therefore, might look like this:

* *Interview.*
* *First letter.* No more than a week later. Thank prospect for his time; summarize meeting, and what benefits prospect can gain doing business with you.
* *First phone call.* "Did you get my letter? Do you have any questions?" Try to eliminate objections through questions and avoid being too pushy.
* *Second letter.* Short, more personal than the first. Say something like, "I look forward to working with you." Attempt to become a friend, someone who is trying to help the prospect.
* *Second phone call.* A critical call. A time to push for the business, without being pushy. "Well, what do you think? Do you have any questions? Are there any problems you see in the proposal?" Ask these important questions and wait patiently for an answer. Then be ready to counter objections.

If no sale occurs after this phone call,
or no definitive action is promised you,
then you must begin again.

* *Third letter.* Thank your prospect once again for considering your company. Say that you are still looking forward to doing business, and that you'll call soon to see when you can get together to discuss it in person.

*Remember—greater sales are awarded to
those who persist. Excellent follow-up is excellent
persistence, and could be your personal turning point
in selling.*

In a very real sense, the follow-up process can be compared to the most memorable experience you could have dining in a fine restaurant. Think of the waiter as the salesman. His job is to be there to answer your questions, to present the available entrées in a pleasant way, to fill your water glass, to bring you more coffee, to show you the dessert menu. What he should not do is be obvious. He should not hover, or be there every time you look up. If he is, the chances are that you will become distracted from your dinner conversation, annoyed with everything about the restaurant, and never come back.

But if he does everything he is supposed to do, services you throughout the meal without your ever giving him more than a second thought, then he has probably (assuming you like the food) sold you on his restaurant and given you a wonderful dining experience that you almost certainly will relay to other potential customers.

And so it is with the salesman who learns to use successful verbal and written follow-up techniques on his prospects and future customers. If he follows up with his customers with skill, grace, and a sensitivity to their needs and agenda, he will enjoy a great feast of personal reward and satisfaction far greater than he imagined possible.

Ten

Put Rejection
to Work for You

Failure is, in a sense, the highway to success, inasmuch as every discovery of what is false leads us to seek earnestly after what is true, and every fresh experience points out some form of error which we shall afterward carefully avoid.

Keats

He only is exempt from failures who makes no efforts.

Whately

He is a best-selling author who has written *Restoring the American Dream* and *Winning Through Intimidation*. His name is Robert Ringer, and if book sales are any gauge of a person's acceptance, he has a huge following of people who embrace his ideas. Yet Ringer advocates the very thing that makes mediocre salespeople out of many who might otherwise have been brilliant, and failed salespeople out of those who might have been very successful in selling, but never really gave it a chance because they allowed their early sales rejection to get them down, and eventually out of selling.

Through his "Theory of Sustenance of a Positive Attitude Through the Assumption of a Negative Result" (explained in *Winning Through Intimidation*), Ringer epitomizes just what is wrong with many who call themselves professional salespeople. He says, "This theory doesn't mean that a person should enter a sales situation (almost any situation in life can be classified as a 'sales situation') feeling that he can't make the sale. What he should do is realistically assume that he won't make the sale." Ringer goes on to say that you should go into the selling situation prepared and confident, "but realistically assuming the worst . . . simply because . . . no matter how well prepared you are, only a small percentage of deals actually close."[1]

To this "assume you will fail" principle, I say baloney! To go into selling with this negative assumption can be the kiss of death for most salespeople. Just think about what it means to assume you're not going to close the deal even before you have the interview. This "wrongheaded" type of thinking can affect you in so many ways.

He's not going to buy anyway, so maybe you'll leave just a little later for your appointment, have one more cup of coffee. So you're late. You're relaxed—because he's not going to buy—so you give your presentation smoothly, almost mechanically. You're really boring because you don't have that extra edge. You're not as concerned with eye contact—after all, he's not going to buy—so you don't pick up the fact that he stopped looking at you and is now gazing distractedly at the picture behind you on the far wall, stopping every now and then to look at his watch. Soon, you're ushered politely out of his office with no challenges, no questions, no dialogue of any kind—and no sale—because you lacked the hypersensitivity that salespeople must have, the "radar" they must turn on to sense when things aren't going right, when they are not giving the prospect what he wants. And all because you became a mechanical salesperson, because you "assumed failure" instead of success, and were rewarded with a self-fulfilling prophecy.

The tragedy is that many salespeople who have never heard of Robert Ringer set themselves up for this kind of failure every day of their selling lives. They can't handle rejection, for whatever reason, and instead of working through what at the time seems like an impossible hurdle for the greater success that lays beyond, they take the low road, accepting no for an answer and settling for whatever level is safest, easiest, and least troublesome.

The Big Difference Between
Rejection and Failure

There is great irony here in that those who have been most successful in sales, who have achieved their sales goals and continue to set new, higher goals, know all about rejection and failure and have had to battle through many personal sales setbacks to achieve what they set out to do. They view rejections as only temporary roadblocks, or impediments in the way of the sale they know they are going to eventually make. Failure is never considered until all possible sales closes have been explored. And even then—after an accumulation of rejections has turned into a failure—it is viewed in the best possible way:

everything was done that could possibly be done. "And after all," these never-say-diers reason, "maybe they'll buy in a few months." Make no mistake—this is no Pollyanna approach, only a tough, persistent "never give up" attitude—an assumption of success, not of failure.

For when you get down to it, sales rejections and occasional failures (which I define as when you don't make the sale) are as much a part of selling as overcoming objections, closing the sale, and the ultimate success that comes with that closing. Yet the amount of contemporary sales literature showing salespeople how to deal with this "dark side" of selling is scarce, focusing instead on the more positive aspects of how to sell and be successful at it.

Rather than dwell on the negative and take the "assume to fail" approach, the following pages will offer some thoughts and helpful ideas about how to work successfully through rejection and failure, the two-headed dragon that all salespeople must ultimately face.

Rejection Doesn't Mean You Are a Failure

Rejection, psychologists tell us, is one of the toughest things we will have to deal with in our lives. It can cause all sorts of negative feelings—depression, anxiety, and self-doubt are just a few. And yet, people who attempt to sell anything—product, service, soliciting funds for charity, etc.—must put up with fairly regular doses of rejection, and learn how not to let it get them down.

It is true that rejection of salespeople by their prospects can and does occur every day for very understandable reasons. The salesman can fail to do the very basic things that he must do before he has a chance to get his story accepted. He can be perpetually late to most of his appointments. He can lack sensitivity and never be tuned in to his prospect, which in turn can cause him to miss some vital signals being transmitted: body language, objection to key points he has made, a silent, nonresponsive attitude. He doesn't communicate between interviews. He fails to send the prospect requested information, or to get back to him at a prearranged time. The number of reasons for rejection are almost as numerous as those for acceptance, and have much to do with how the salesman treats his prospect. If the prospect is made to feel important, if his time and needs are honored and respected by the salesman, then this very basic kind of rejection should never happen.

It is when the salesman has done everything he has to do to secure a sale (he thinks), and then is rejected, that the greatest amount of frustration and depression is most likely to set in. Negative thoughts can poison what should be an optimistic, enthusiastic spirit. "Why didn't he buy? I did everything I was supposed to do. What a great deal I gave him—and he still didn't buy. I can't understand people like that. He must have been unconscious when I showed him how much his profits could increase if he installed our system." You've heard this sad refrain before. Maybe you've uttered it yourself. But in selling, it is deadly to allow the Ultimate Rejection—a sales failure—to get you down. Shake it off, be content that you have done everything possible to make the sale, and then come back with this rule firmly in your mind:

*A rejection is only a temporary setback—
it is not a failure of the individual.*

Working Through Rejection to Success

The fact is that everyone, regardless of profession, is rejected and experiences failure in their lives. But not everyone tries to sell something, and therefore may not experience the mountain of rejection that salespeople can experience as they pursue their careers day in, day out.

During a seminar I attended recently, John Johnson, one of the most successful businessmen in America and founder of *Ebony* magazine, recounted his early struggles in attempting to solicit major advertising accounts for his fledgling magazine:

> The Leo Burnett Advertising Agency had several key accounts we were pursuing, but with absolutely no success. Every salesman who went after their business, including me, was rejected. But we were all unanimous in our feeling that we were never considered very seriously, that no one really listened very well to our concept. I decided I had nothing to lose, so I requested a personal meeting with Leo Burnett himself. He listened very carefully to my story and said, "Mr. Johnson, I can't guarantee I can get my executives to buy advertising in your magazine, but I *can* guarantee they'll listen to your story." And from that point on, we were taken seriously by the Burnett agency, and ultimately established a solid business relationship with them.

Johnson persisted. He worked through his early rejections, analyzed what he thought was wrong, and went in another direction. He took his case right to the top, and this time it paid off in the success he was looking for.

In his book *Discover Your Possibilities*, The Reverend Robert H. Schuller summarized this never-say-die approach to failure:

> How do you handle your past failures? Suppose you tried again and again but failed. What does that mean? Failure doesn't mean you'll never make it. It does mean you have to do it differently.[2]

The key for anyone, especially salespeople, is not to take rejection or failure personally. As Pete Lakey, successful business consultant and former top executive with a major pharmaceutical company, says, "You should always look at failure when it happens—and it will—as an individual failure, not a failure of the individual."

That many salespeople never allow themselves to experience success because they get mired down in rejection is to me one of the saddest aspects of my profession. I have seen good, enthusiastic salespeople armed with a solid knowledge of a product leave the selling profession as quickly as they entered it, their train to success and a good income derailed by repeated *nos*, unkind words, objections of all sorts, simply because they didn't know how to handle these walls of resistance. As Skip Ross says in his excellent little book *Say Yes to Your Potential*, that is definitely the wrong way to look at defeat.

> A temporary setback is not a total knockout. There is nothing wrong or disgraceful about getting knocked down. Virtually all the greats have experienced temporary defeats. Those are the learning times, the opportunities for you to grow and achieve your destiny. If you get up one more time than you fall, you will make it through.[3]

What is your attitude toward failure or sales rejection? If you never thought too much about it, or put it out of your mind because it sounds negative, think of it in another way. Are you surprised by your own success? If so, then maybe you have set yourself up to fail on a regular basis, because it's more comfortable, less challenging than success, certainly easier to attain. As my friend Dave Grant is fond of saying to the hundreds of people in church and professional groups he lectures to every year, "Tell me what surprises you, and I'll tell you what you believe."

Learn to Reject Rejection and Get
Back to Basics

In other words, be as surprised by the failures you encounter as the successes you achieve. Be surprised but not upset, challenged but not discouraged. When you have made thirty-five phone calls in a day with absolutely no success, try a thirty-sixth. It could be the payoff you were looking for.

In Britain's darkest hours, when the Germans were winning World War II, Winston Churchill was that country's living symbol of strength, determination, and persistence against incredible odds. A political failure himself in the years before the war, Churchill refused to give up and eventually a wounded nation called on him to lead her out of the abyss. After the war, he was an international hero and a gifted speaker and he gave one of his most famous speeches—and certainly one of the shortest ever on record—at commencement exercises for Oxford University. "Never give up" was the first line . . . and the second line . . . and the third and last line, spoken dramatically at several-second intervals, each time received with thundering applause. It was the mark of the man and his success in life that he refused to allow failure, rejection, and defeat after defeat to get him down. He rejected rejection outright, and would only accept victory. There simply was no alternative.

To put Churchill's philosophy into a direct-selling situation is not to demean or trivialize the enormity of the task he faced. More specifically, it is Churchill's attitude that salesmen can learn from. To be prepared, to plan for success, to assume success, to work as hard as you can to achieve success, and then to persist in the face of rejection after rejection—that is the lesson for salespeople who study Churchill.

Echoing Churchill's philosophy is Norman Vincent Peale,

who in his classic *Power of Positive Thinking* had this to say
about obstacles:

> The first thing to do about an obstacle is simply to stand
> up to it and not complain about it or whine under it but
> forthrightly attack it. Don't go crawling through life on
> your hands and knees half-defeated. Stand up to your ob-
> stacles and do something about them. You will find that
> they haven't half the strength you think they have.[4]

Think You'll Sell Everyone, Instead of Doubting You'll Sell Anyone

Demonstrating this kind of dogged persistence was a top automobile salesman I had a conversation with the other day. "I
had a terrible first six months this year," he was saying. "It was
like I was out of sync with my customers. I just couldn't get
anybody to buy in the numbers I was used to. And what was
worse, everyone else around me was cleaning up. Our dealership had more sales than any other dealership in Southern California. It was literally raining sales, and I was walking through
the raindrops without getting a drop on me." What did my
salesman friend do? "Well, I didn't give up, although I was
pretty discouraged. I knew I had to get back to the basics, to
what I was doing before when I was doing so well. So I made a
list of all the sales arguments I thought I had memorized. I
surprised myself, because there were a couple on the list I had
been leaving out. Then I decided to come in an hour earlier
and leave an hour later. Finally, I just assumed I was going to
sell everyone who came through the door. Soon, my sales
began to pick up and it looks as though I'm going to finish the
year as the top salesman again. The reason for my turnaround?

I just couldn't believe I had lost my touch, that I could be that bad all of a sudden. I worked hard, refused to accept my mediocre performance, and got back to the basics. That's all it seemed to take."

Although my car-salesman friend worked through his series of failures, he did have a big edge. He had been very successful before, so knowing what it took to get him there the first time, he merely went back to that formula. That he felt confident enough to go back to what had worked for him before is a reflection of his positive attitude toward selling, what most often makes the difference in success or failure, according to W. Clement Stone, one of the most successful insurance entrepreneurs in the country and founder of *Success* magazine. Stone, commenting in his book *The Success System That Never Fails*, says, "The more I search to discover the powers of the human mind and how to use them, the more I am convinced that success or failure is primarily the result of the attitude of the individual."[5] Summing up this kind of thinking is Joe Girard, acknowledged to be one of the greatest car salesmen of all time. Girard says:

> You are thinking most positively when you believe that you should be able to sell everybody who comes in. Realistically, of course, nobody can do that. But it is still a very effective attitude to have. It encourages you to analyze every lost sale to see why you lost it so that you can try to correct the mistake next time you run into the same kind of situation.[6]

Regardless of experience or past success, learn to develop that winning attitude—to accept that rejection and failure will come as a part of your taking a greater risk by asking all kinds of people every day to buy something you are selling. The law of averages says you will not make every sale, just as it says a baseball player will not hit every pitch that is thrown to him. But if you keep swinging, you'll get your share of hits, and in the process illustrate a rule for dealing with rejection that can be put this way:

Success is often a step from rejection: take that step, and succeed!

How to Hurdle the Rejection Roadblock

Learning to develop the right attitude about rejection and sales failures is really only half the battle. The truly successful salesperson needs to know how to respond to rejections when they occur. He should have the ability to cope with rejection, and also the ability to attack it—to recognize why it happened and develop strategies for overcoming it. Rejection, then, is only a temporary setback, a roadblock in the normal selling process for which there is a detour that will put the salesman back on the road to success again.

Let's look at it another way. Experienced salespeople know the pitfalls of selling their products. They've been rejected before, know what arguments they're likely to face, and prepare counterarguments before they have their interviews. They're really playing chess with prospects as they sit down in the relative quiet of their offices, planning strategy before interviews. "If I say *A*, he's liable to object with *B*, in which case I can give him the *C* counterargument." These people are planning to hurdle the rejection roadblock before it comes up—a vital strategy for all successful salespeople to adopt.

While on a business trip recently, I happened to sit next to another author on the plane who expressed a real interest in the subject of this chapter. "A friend of mine is a very successful land salesman for lakefront property," said my traveling companion. "One day I asked him how he became the top salesman in his company, and he had a very interesting answer. He told me that he always thought he was a natural salesman, and was enjoying average success, but became bothered by the mounting number of rejections he was receiving. His income began to suffer and although he never talked about his business at home, one day he became so frustrated that he blurted out to his wife the story of what he perceived to be his failures in selling. He then began to go through the typical sales approach he had been using, and by the time he was finished, he was really finished! I mean, she just shot his pitch full of holes. I guess he had been living on old information and the same old story for so long that it hadn't dawned on him how weak and unconvincing his sales presentation had become. Well, from that point on, he was a changed salesman. Now he studies his industry regularly and develops new presentations every few weeks, completely revamping his pitch. And he *always* tries his new presentation out on his toughest critic—his wife—before he takes it to his first potential customer. He changes even the smallest flaw in it, and then he's ready. And to this point, it's been almost all success."

What our land salesman learned and freely recognized from his wife was the mediocrity of his overall effort. His pitch had grown stale, so had he, and his sales had plummeted accordingly. But out of this failure, he learned to try his presentation on his toughest critic (in this case, his wife) and let her be an independent judge of the strength or weakness of his various sales arguments. He was listening for rejection when it didn't really matter, when the sale wasn't on the line, when he could adapt and make his arguments stronger. He was practicing a rule that is a key to overcoming rejection roadblocks before they happen. That rule can be stated this way:

Learn to practice strategic rejection.

Dr. Alan Loy McGinnis has appeared in over three hundred radio, television, and newspaper interviews since the publication of his first book, *The Friendship Factor*, over seven years ago. Yet as experienced and as polished a media guest as he is now, I'll never forget how apprehensive he was prior to his first media book-promotion tour. Nervous, but very smart, because he recognized how little he knew about promoting his book via media interviews. Well, he invited the Somdals over one evening and after dinner I developed some questions for a "practice" interview, which we conducted in the living room with our families as the audience. In retrospect, some of the questions I fired at him were overly harsh and probably never in danger of being asked, yet he often mentioned later how important that tough little interview was in preparing him for the many interviews, some of them very tough, he was to face later in the promotion of his three books.

A word about your "practice adversary": Not everyone has the ability—or desire—to include their spouses in their business affairs. Whoever it is—business associate, close friend, relative, or spouse—the principal goal here is to "try out" your sales pitch with a significant other person. *Important:* Do not pick a pussycat to listen to your presentation. If you're looking for instant acceptance, to feel good about the brilliance of your strategy, you are missing the whole point. Remember—you want to win the final test, you want to make the sale, and to do that you need to get yourself ready for any rejection that might

occur with the strongest possible sales approach, including answers and counteranswers to all possible sales objections you
and your practice adversary can think of.

Some Positive "Be-Attitudes" for Conquering Rejection

I must conclude this chapter on rejection with some of the
things I think you must "be" when faced with what appears to
be a stone wall of opposition, attitudes I have found helpful in
my bleakest sales hours:

1. *Be angry—and channel that anger.* Although anger is normally not an emotion I would ever suggest any salesperson
   regularly employ, it can be helpful at certain moments. For
   example, let's say you've just been turned down for a key account you know you should have sold, have worked months
   to achieve, and suddenly find it's gone to the opposition. If
   you care—I mean, really care—you'll get over any short-term
   depression you may feel and take the "that's my account—
   what are they doing with it?" attitude. It's as though the fox
   has gotten in the hen house and taken your chicken. You actually take ownership of the account you haven't sold, and
   through a positive channeling of your anger over this "great
   injustice," you become sharper and more clearly focused on
   what it is you have to do to sell the account. As my friend
   Dr. Neil Warren says it in his excellent book *Make Anger
   Your Ally,* "You can use your anger constructively. In fact,
   you can become the master of your own anger! ... If you
   learn to take full advantage of your anger, it can help you discover the deepest and most satisfying levels of meaning, both
   in relationship to others and to yourself."[7] Get angry when
   you are rejected because that business belongs to you. And
   then channel your anger into a constructive plan to get it.

2. *Be determined.* Very little of what we do can take the place of determination, the sheer desire to achieve a goal no matter how hard, how far away, or how many seemingly insurmountable obstacles get in the way. Americans love people who have succeeded in spite of the rejections and failures they encountered along the way, and history is replete with such examples of fierce determination. Our founding fathers determined to secure liberty even if it meant fighting the most powerful nation on the earth at that time. Abraham Lincoln determined to hold the union together in the face of failure after failure from his army and very little popular support at home. Franklin Roosevelt's ironclad resolve pulled an economically battered nation out of the worst depression the world had ever seen. That these men etched a place in history for themselves is important because of the tremendous odds against them, and their determination to overcome those odds. When rejections pile up and your task seems impossible, buoy yourself up with the inspiration of others and the knowledge that you will eventually succeed if you are determined to succeed.

3. *Be persistent.* If determination is the will to win, persistence is putting that will into action. One of the most determined, persistent people I have ever known is a young boy I coached in soccer a few years ago. At an age when most boys were either hitting, bouncing, or kicking a ball during most of their waking moments, Robert (not his real name) did not have the coordination necessary to kick an unmoving soccer ball. And while he improved greatly during the course of the season, it was the last game of the season I remember most. The ball went out of bounds right by me, and one of the more coordinated boys and Robert both ran over to throw it in. The other boy grabbed it out of Robert's hands, and was about to throw it in when Robert gave me a pleading look. He actually wanted the ball. There's a correct way to throw the ball in or the other team takes possession, and common

sense told me to let the other boy throw it in. But Robert's desire, his determination in that look, really got to me, so I told the other boy to get in the game and let Robert throw the ball in. Well, that throw was perfect, as were the next five I let Robert throw in, and although we only won two games and lost nine that season, I know that for one uncoordinated but determined and persistent little kid named Robert, the year had ended in a rousing success. As Calvin Coolidge so eloquently put it, "Nothing in the world can take the place of persistence. Talent will not. Nothing is more common than unsuccessful men with talent. Genius will not. Unrewarded genius is almost a proverb. Education will not. The world is full of educated derelicts. Persistence, determination, and hard work make the difference."

4. *Be analytical.* After the rejection, have the courage to face up to the situation. Why did you fail to make the sale? What was it that you said, or did—didn't do, or didn't say? Was there something mechanical in your delivery that contributed to your rejection? Was it just bad timing? Rather than second-guessing yourself, you are attempting to learn from your experience, to separate the positives from the negatives. If you need to, write the pluses and minuses down in two columns on a piece of paper. Then, after you've analyzed the meeting you were just in, write down the action you are going to take to make sure that whatever deficiencies you detected are corrected in your next presentation. If you find it impossible to analyze your own failings—and many people do—then definitely seek help. And do it before it's too late. What good does it do to be consistently rejected and realize you should have asked for help before you were fired? Go to the sales manager or whoever is your boss early. Don't expect him to come to you. Tell him you'd like to practice a little "strategic rejection" by giving him the sales pitch you just had rejected. He should admire your desire to practice and

could possibly correct what you are doing wrong in very short order.

5. *Be confident you'll come back.* Perhaps the most difficult quality to infuse in any salesperson is confidence, especially after a rejection. Just getting dressed to go to work can be difficult, getting out to see the same kinds of people who just rejected you an impossibility. Yet if you are ever going to succeed in selling, just after you have experienced a failure is precisely the time you should bear down and work harder than you have before. For if you become afraid, if you become "call reluctant," if you do nothing because you are afraid to fail, precisely nothing will happen. But if you are confident that success will come your way if you work hard and learn from past failures—that failure of any kind is merely an aberration, and that success is really the norm for you—then you will be able to put your temporary rejections and rare failures behind you and proceed with the success you know you are entitled to.

Confront your rejection, attack your failure, and you will become one of those rare people who wear the mantle of success with grace and dignity because they would not settle for the ease of failure and were not afraid to do the hard work necessary for success. As W. Clement Stone says:

> Do what you're afraid to do . . . go where you're afraid to go . . . when you run away because you are afraid to do something big, you pass opportunity by.[8]

Eleven

The Power of
Saying Thanks

Two kinds of gratitude: the sudden kind we feel for what we take, the larger kind we feel for what we give.

E.A. Robinson

The deepest principle in human nature is the craving to be appreciated.

William James

What I shall always remember about meeting Lee Booth on the short flight from North Carolina to New York City is his story of Jim Easter. Lee is a top executive from Lane Furniture

171

Company, and while we talked about a variety of subjects, naturally the topic of sales came up.

"You asked who the best salesman in our company is," he said, repeating my question. "That is Jim Easter, hands down. And he doesn't work in L.A. or New York or even close to any big metropolitan city. What's so amazing is that he does this phenomenal volume in Oklahoma. That's his territory—smaller than most major metropolitan cities—and yet he is our leading sales producer." Lee leaned closer to make an important point. "And you know what the secret to his success is?" He paused, relishing his question, his eyes intent on mine, convinced I couldn't guess Jim's secret.

He was right. "I give up," I said.

"He simply thanks everyone for everything, wherever he goes," Lee said. "That's it—*he thanks people.*"

I must have shown some astonishment at such a simplistic answer, for as if reading my mind, Lee came right back to offer some additional insight into this super salesman. "Of course Jim's a great talker. He is also an ordained minister in the Episcopal church. But honestly, it's amazing. I've seen it as I've ridden around on calls with him. He really is a grateful person and he shows it, thanking prospects for their business—sometimes even before he gets it—and always for their time. No matter what the situation, he always finds some reason to thank them. And then, when they place their order, I've often seen him tell customers they shouldn't buy that much for their size store, that he would feel more comfortable with a smaller order for now, and that he'll certainly sell them more if they need more. Well, that flabbergasts them for sure—a salesman advising them not to buy so much. But you know, they sincerely appreciate his integrity and always follow his thanks with their own heartfelt gratitude. Of course, almost all of Jim's customers continue to buy more from him year after year."

As I reflected on this wonderful story, I couldn't help but think how Jim Easter had his priorities solidly in order, and that he recognized how much he had to be thankful for. And while I've never met Jim Easter, I could imagine him extending one more set of thanks, in one of his churches on Sunday morning, to God for giving him such a rich and full life.

Gratitude: A Gift That Always Gives Back

Have you followed Jim Easter's path, and given the gift of gratitude to any of your prospects or customers lately? If not, why not? It's one of the few gifts I know of that is universally appreciated and almost always reciprocated. Yet for some reason, it often is ignored by members of the professional selling fraternity who should know better. Dale Carnegie summarized the great value of this seldom-practiced attitude beautifully when he said:

> One of the most neglected virtues of our daily existence is appreciation. Somehow, we neglect to praise our son or daughter when he or she brings home a good report card, and we fail to encourage our children when they first succeed in baking a cake or building a birdhouse. Nothing pleases children more than this kind of parental interest and approval.

> The next time you enjoy filet mignon at the club, send word to the chef that it was excellently prepared, and when a tired salesman shows you unusual courtesy, please mention it. . . . In our interpersonal relations we should never forget that all our associates are human beings and hunger for appreciation. It is the legal tender that all souls enjoy.[1]

One person who knows the value and the power of giving thanks on a regular basis is Ira Pavon, our home and auto insurance representative. A few days after he had made a presentation to me on an interesting new life insurance program, I received in the mail some additional details on the policy, and a personal thank-you note from Ira. It was the end of the day; I was tired and didn't really want to deal with the details of the policy, so I set it aside. But I read the thank-you note because it was short and personal. Here is what it said:

> Thank you for discussing your insurance with me recently.
>
> Your courtesy is sincerely appreciated and you may be sure I will respect it by providing you with the best service I can.

The note was signed personally by Ira, and when he called me the next day to see if I had received the policy details, I greeted him warmly and thanked him for his kindness. He said the thank-you note was his own idea, and that he had a large quantity of them printed at his own expense because he felt it was important to let people know how much he appreciated their time.

Ira's life insurance program is excellent, but what stands out is his thoughtfulness, expressed in a brief message on a little card. I will probably give Ira some additional business because he has set himself apart in the insurance world where one program often blends into another with no discernible difference. He has proven himself to be one who truly values his customers and their time—and tells them so.

One final word: While Ira's expressed motive for preparing and sending his little thank-you notes is contained in the message itself, there can be no doubt that as an excellent salesperson, he is keenly aware of the note's reciprocal business value. Or to put it simply, he sincerely thanks people for their time and is often rewarded with more business. Certainly this doesn't always happen, but the "give and you shall receive" concept is an important principle that is practiced by thoughtful, caring people both in and out of business.

This concept was the subject of a sermon preached just recently by our minister, the Reverend Donn Moomaw, pastor of Bel Air Presbyterian Church. In a powerful moment during the message dealing with the reciprocity of giving, Reverend Moomaw declared, "The old rock sitting in the sun doesn't give back its own warmth—it gives back the warmth it received from the sun."

Are you generating genuine warmth and enthusiasm by thanking people for the opportunities they have given you? Or are you going about your business pursuing everything you can get, with no concern about something so mundane as a "thank you," waiting instead for someone to warm your heart with a thank you before you might respond in kind? I sincerely hope not. I hope you are not waiting, like the rock, to feel the warmth. Instead, try spreading some warmth yourself. And do it now! You know how much you love to be appreciated. So why not be a self-starter and see what great rewards you will receive. This principle can be summarized:

Give your wholehearted appreciation,
and you will receive more than you give.

Network Your Thanks to Others

Anyone who follows Oscar night on television and watches the parade of stars who come to the microphone to accept their coveted awards (while giving endless thanks to everyone) also knows the standard joke associated with the whole process: "I'd especially like to thank my father and my mother, without whom none of this would have been possible."

After an entire evening of thank yous, year after year, they do seem redundant and cliché-ridden, even to many in the movie industry. But lest we get too jaded, let's examine the dynamics of what is really going on here. The Motion Picture Academy is thanking its own for doing their best work. And in turn, while the award winners are basically thanking a list of people we have never heard of, they are really taking advantage of a gigantic nationwide forum to announce their deep gratitude to their peers in what is a very small industry with a short memory. Without commenting on the sincerity of each thank you, the point is that members of the motion picture industry know the value of saying thanks when the opportunity arises.

The Los Angeles Dodgers draw over three million customers per year and are without question the most successful, well-run organization in baseball. So with their pockets bulging and continued prospects of more of the same for years to come, why would this most successful business take full-page ads in daily newspapers throughout Southern California, spending thousands of dollars on these ads at the end of the 1985 baseball season? Because they wanted to give thanks to their baseball fans, the people without whom there would be no successful Los Angeles Dodgers baseball organization. The ad showed a picture of the entire Dodger ballclub, and carried a very simple but heartfelt message: "Thank You for Sharing a Great Season. The Los Angeles Dodgers." What a great way to show appreciation to millions of fans who picked up their papers that morning and were rewarded with a special, personal thank-you note from a grateful team.

You don't have to take a full-page ad, or win an Oscar on

nationwide television to network your thanks. It's much simpler than that. All you need do is be sensitive and responsive to as many people as possible—preferably everyone you meet—and you will soon see the power of networking your thanks unfold. Tom Hopkins, the tremendously successful sales trainer, lecturer, and author, learned how rapidly a thank you can be spread at an early stage in his career, as this story illustrates:

> When I cashed my first sizable check in sales, I went right out and bought a suit because I needed clothes desperately. During the next few days that suit got a lot of wear. Then it had a collision with a gob of oil. When I rushed my suit to the cleaners, the owner of the shop rushed it out in time for my next appointment. So I wrote him a thank-you note that he taped on the front of his cash register along with my business card. Three days later I got a call from another customer of his who'd seen my note. That call led to a large sale. Besides putting a chunk of money in my pocket, that incident taught me a lesson.
>
> Thank people. Do it in writing. And do it right away.[2]

It is clear that you can see positive results by networking your gratitude—that is, sharing your appreciation with as wide an audience as possible. Most successful volunteer groups realized that a long time ago, and have perfected the art of networking their thanks by way of mass mailings, television and radio commercials, newspaper ads, and fund-raising dinners and performances. Along with everyone else who networks their enthusiasm and gratitude, this fundamental principle works for groups and individuals alike:

Show your thanks immediately and
to as many people as possible.

A Short Course in Expressing Gratitude

The meeting was over, signified by the secretary's second impatient buzz on the intercom, and as I rose to go I was about to thank my gracious host for his time in giving me the interview when he spoke first.

"I greatly appreciate the time you have spent to come and talk to me today," he said, grasping my hand warmly. "I hope we can do this again soon."

Amazed—because as the salesman trying to sell this senior vice-president advertising in my newspaper I was in his debt for *his* time and trouble—I managed "you're welcome," along with my own sincere thanks for the time he spent listening to my proposal. After I got into a cab on the crowded New York street, I felt a sort of warm glow as I went over what this busy, high-level executive had just done for me and for my opinion of him. No matter what the business outcome of the meeting—although it turned out very positively for both businesses—this encounter had become for me a high point of that particular sales trip because of the appreciation he showed for my time. He had given me a gift—the gift of thanks—which in turn gave me an extra charge of enthusiasm every time I worked with him or anyone in his company. He had learned early how to put into practice the art of sincerely giving thanks, and it added an extra human dimension of understanding to his powerful and somewhat awesome position.

The fine art of giving gratitude should be learned and practiced for every human endeavor, whether you are a guest or the host, buying or selling. There are a few important things you can learn about the practice of giving thanks during selling situations, and I offer them for your consideration here:

1. *Recognize when people are extending themselves for you.* If a prospect has squeezed you into his or her busy day due to your "brilliant salesmanship," don't waste time patting yourself on the back. Thank your prospect and do it as soon as you are ushered into his office. As you are sitting down, say something like, "I really appreciate the time you've made available when I know it's a tough time for you. I'm going to keep this very brief, just hitting the most important points, in the interest of your time." After you've said that—that is, acknowledged how busy and important his day is—an amazing thing might happen: *you* might be told to "relax and take your time," or asked if you would like a cup of coffee, or extended ten minutes beyond the time the prospect said he had with his own questions. And I am absolutely convinced that it all starts with a sincere thank you for his sharing some of his valuable time with you. Also learn to recognize when your prospect sneaks a furtive look at his watch, and immediately address it with a thank you and a request for two more minutes to summarize. You will almost always get at least five minutes, because you were kind enough to recognize that your interview time was up.

2. *Say thanks because you mean it.* On the surface, this point seems self-explanatory, but there is a danger of underestimating the great value of this simple line. Do you sincerely appreciate the things that have been given you? And can you transfer that sincerity to your selling situations, without seeming forced or affected? Expressing sincere gratitude means the difference between appreciation and flattery. Most people know the difference and will gratefully accept one while tolerating the other. And the difference is really a reflection of what is felt deep within you. "Thank you" can be a powerful reciprocal gift when it is sincerely given, or it can be flat and ineffective when it is given as the last item on a list of things you ought to do.

3. *Thank people in person when possible.* These days, it seems that close personal relationships are at a premium. As a nation, we always seem to be breathlessly on our way somewhere and then, when we get there, we need to keep a sharp eye on our watch for the next place we have to visit by a certain time. Salespeople often lead a life like that, especially if they are working on a commission basis. There never seem to be enough hours in the day to make sales calls, and certainly not enough to make service calls—that is, calling on the account when he is already sold. But that is often the most important time to call—when you have the business and have an excellent rapport.

That's the time to cement the relationship with a personal thank you—dropping by the client's office to say "hello and thanks for the business" and to check to see if he needs anything; a lunch invitation just because you appreciate the business; hand delivering a small gift—flowers, a plant, candy—to commemorate some special day (the first-year anniversary of your doing business together, a special promotion the client may have received, etc.). The main point about a personal thank you is that you took the time to be there. (Note: If you can't say thanks in person, by all means don't delay saying thanks on the phone or with a short note—but whenever possible, do it in person. It shows how much you really care).

4. *Say thanks even after a cold reception.* Without doubt, one of the toughest times to show appreciation is when you feel as though you haven't been appreciated. The person you have attempted to persuade has kept you waiting an hour, and then has seen you for only five minutes; your presentation was interrupted by ten phone calls and people barging into the office every two minutes; your prospect actually resents seeing you and to make that point is combative and surly throughout your presentation.

Whatever the situation—from cold indifference to out-right hostility—it almost never pays to allow yourself to sink to the level of the treatment you are receiving. To do so only lends credence and justification to the way the prospect has been treating you. On the contrary, it is during times like these when you need to rise to the occasion and show your genuine appreciation for the time the prospect has made available, thank him for his thoughtful consideration of your proposal, and tell him you will call to see what he has decided when his schedule is less hectic.

Make no mistake—this advice is difficult to accept. It is far more normal to want to get in there and mix it up with your adversary. But learn to give him the benefit of the doubt during difficult interviews. After all, maybe he has had a bad day, has tons of work to do with little time to finish it, or doesn't feel well. I have learned over a period of time to judge people on the "long haul" and to really believe I can sell anyone eventually. Therefore, emotions aside, "thank you" is now much easier to say on a regular basis, regardless of the outcome of the meeting.

The important thing, in developing an ease in saying thanks, is to remember and consider the other people involved, their agendas and their own busy lives. Learn to enjoy your interview time with your prospects and develop the facility to put yourself in their place, and you will grow rapidly in your sensitivity.

There Are Always Reasons to Give Thanks

To the beleaguered salesman who has just suffered through a series of sales setbacks, or who has been rejected for the "nth" time, that "there are always reasons to be thankful" seems like easy advice to give but extremely hard to take. "What is there to give thanks for when my luck is so rotten, or I've just lost a big account?" the question might go. If you've ever experienced a down time like that—and who hasn't—it is difficult to disagree with the intensity and power of these kinds of negative emotions, especially when it appears you've done more than enough to succeed and still come up empty.

But the real question here is not whether or not you've been treated fairly. The question is how much remorse and negative energy are you willing to invest into a situation that is beyond your control? And how much faith do you have that you will eventually turn things around ... that your situation will and must improve, because it certainly couldn't get any worse? These questions are critical to every human being, but especially pertinent to the salesman who must have faith in the future to pick himself up and carry on in spite of adversity.

I sincerely believe in the power of this kind of faith and "inventory analysis" of what you have and where you are. This was a lesson learned early by W. Clement Stone, nationally known insurance executive and editor and publisher of *Success* magazine. Stone tells of a time when, while vacationing with his family in Florida, he received a telegram from the president of a large eastern accident-and-health-insurance company he represented, saying that within two weeks his services would no longer be needed. The jobs of over a thousand agents, as well as the viability of Stone's company, hinged on this account. The president of the company was on a world tour and couldn't be reached. What would you do in such a situation? The temptation to be depressed or panicky, to give up and contemplate bankruptcy, would be great—the easy way out— and most people might have made that decision. But not Stone, a man who refused to give up. Here is what he did, in his own words:

> I told no one, but cloistered myself in my bedroom for 45
> minutes. I reasoned: God is always a good God; right is
> right; and with every disadvantage there is a greater ad-
> vantage, if one seeks and finds it. Then I knelt down and
> thanked God for my blessings: a healthy body, a healthy
> mind, a wonderful wife and three wonderful children, the
> privilege of living in this great land of freedom—this land
> of unlimited opportunity—and the joy of being alive. I
> prayed for guidance. I prayed for help. And I *believed*
> that I would receive them.[3]

And as he wrote the story, Stone did receive guidance and
help. His prayer and his giving thanks when things looked the
darkest got him into a positive frame of mind to initiate a
course of action and set a list of goals—one of which was to
keep the account from which he had just been fired. He not
only kept the account but he also established his own accident-and-health-insurance company, which eventually grew
into one of the largest in the country. When his professional
situation seemed truly hopeless, Stone looked at all that he had
and was truly thankful. Working from that positive mental and
emotional state, he was able to generate a course of action that
took him far beyond the practical realities of the moment
as he read the potentially devastating news contained in the
telegram.

The Reverend Robert Schuller punctuated the value of giving thanks when it was the last thing most people would do as
he recalled his childhood years during the depression, on his
family's midwestern farm. Mired in the middle of a severe
drought, the nation's midsection was quickly choking to death
as farmer after farmer gave up their farms and called it quits,
unable to grow anything without water. Schuller remembers
the remarkable resilience of his father and how he was always
able to find something for which to give thanks:

If it had been a normal year, my father would have expected to harvest corn that would fill dozens of wagons.
That year, my father harvested barely half a wagon of
corn, grown on a half-acre of ground. In a normal year,
this swampy lot, fed by some mysterious underground
spring, was too wet to produce any fruit at all.

My father had often thought about digging deep into the
plot to drain the subsurface water away. Now in the year
of the drought this small plot of ground was the only
parcel out of 160 acres where the corn had survived . . .

It was but half a wagon of corn.

A total disaster? Not quite. For half a wagon of corn was
better than none at all. In fact, it was equal to the
amount of seed that had been sowed earlier that year. A
total loss? No. We gained nothing. But more importantly
we lost nothing.

I shall never forget my father's dinnertime prayer that
night.

"Dear Lord. I thank You that I have lost nothing this
year. You have given me my seed back. Thank you."[4]

Schuller's father went on to rebuild his farm, even after a
tornado destroyed it and it looked as though he could never
come back. He was sustained by a deep and abiding faith and a
sincere gratitude for everything he had been given. And more
important, he showed that gratitude time and again, when he
gave thanks to God for all he had. He possessed the sustaining
power of an intangible quality—faith in God and gratitude for
His gifts—that gave him the added strength to carry on day

after day, in spite of the overwhelming obstacles that seemed to come at him in an unending stream.

Whatever you're selling, take pride in a job well done. But like Reverend Schuller's father, also know the great energy and peace that can come from acknowledging the help you have had along the way. Remember:

***In good times and bad,
give sincere thanks to a higher authority.***

As someone who makes his living persuading people, I am a firm believer in this credo although I confess I don't practice it as much as I should. I often get carried away in my own self-sufficiency and sales expertise, forgetting that God is always by my side, and that I really couldn't make it without my silent "Sales Manager." And then, when times are tough and there seems to be no way for me to make it happen, I turn to God, thanking Him for what I have while I ask for strength and wisdom to carry me through.

I am writing this last chapter in November, close to Thanksgiving, and am particularly sensitive to the significance of this time for this material. I have so much for which to be thankful—my health, loving and caring family and friends, successful career, a beautiful home. The material things I enjoy, along with a great sense of joy and fulfillment, I owe to my career in selling. I hope you have gained from what I have written and that the experience has been worthwhile for you. I know it has been for me.

Source Notes

Chapter 1
You Can Develop the Power to Persuade

1. Robert L. Shook, *Ten Greatest Salespersons* (New York: Harper & Row, Pubs., Inc., 1980), p. 188.

2. Frank Bettger, *How I Raised Myself From Failure to Success in Selling* (Englewood Cliffs, New Jersey: Prentice Hall, Inc., 1983, pp. 42, 43.

Chapter 2
Surround Yourself With Success

1. Alan Greenberg, "Bracing for the Best," the *Los Angeles Times*, April 29, 1984.

2. Ibid.

3. W. Clement Stone, *The Success System That Never Fails* (Englewood Cliffs, New Jersey: Prentice-Hall, Inc., 1962), p. 17.

4. Bob Grinde, "So You're a Salesman," *A Treasury of Success Unlimited*, edited by Og Mandino (New York: Pocket Books, 1984), p. 224.

5. Donald J. Moine, "Going for the Gold in the Selling Game," *Psychology Today*, March 1984, p. 37.

6. John Wooden and Jack Tobin, *They Call Me Coach* (Waco, Texas: Word Books, 1984).

7. Dr. Harold Blake Walker, "Make the Impossible Your Goal," *Treasury*, p. 210.

Chapter 5
Winning From the Beginning

1. Dr. Alan Loy McGinnis, *The Friendship Factor* (Minneapolis: Augsburg, 1979), p. 9.
2. Robert L. Shook, *Ten Greatest Salespersons* (New York: Harper & Row, Pubs., Inc., 1980), p. 35.
3. Tom Hopkins, *How to Master the Art of Selling* (New York: Warner Books, Inc., 1984), p. 174.

Chapter 6
Compare—Compete—and Convince

1. Dr. Alan Loy McGinnis, *Bringing Out the Best in People* (Minneapolis: Augsburg, 1985), pp. 97, 98.
2. Denis Waitley, *Seeds of Greatness* (Old Tappan, New Jersey: Fleming H. Revell Company, 1983), pp. 199, 200.
3. Steven Flax, "How to Snoop on Your Competitors," *Fortune*, May 14, 1984, p. 28.

Chapter 7
Close In to a *Yes*

1. Zig Ziglar, *Secrets of Closing the Sale* (Old Tappan, New Jersey: Fleming H. Revell Company, 1984), p. 379.
2. Lee Iacocca and William Novak, *Iacocca: An Autobiography* (New York: Bantam Books, 1985), p. 208.
3. N. C. Christensen, "Open That Closed Door—and Sell," *A Treasury of Success Unlimited*, edited by Og Mandino (New York: Pocket Books, 1984), p. 236.
4. Ibid.
5. Dr. Harold Blake Walker, "Make the Impossible Your Goal," *A Treasury of Success Unlimited*, edited by Og Mandino (New York: Pocket Books, 1984), p. 212.

Chapter 8
Coming Back From a *No*

1. Dale Carnegie, *How to Win Friends and Influence People* (New York: Pocket Books, 1982), pp. 117, 118.

2. Frank Beach, Richard Buskirk, Frederick Russell, *Selling: Principles and Practices* (New York: McGraw-Hill, 1982), p. 288.
3. Mitch Polin, the *Los Angeles Times*, October 8, 1985.
4. Ibid.
5. Ibid.

Chapter 10
Put Rejection to Work for You

1. Robert J. Ringer, *Winning Through Intimidation* (New York: Fawcett Book Group, 1979), pp. 22, 23.
2. Robert H. Schuller, *Discover Your Possibilities* (New York: Ballantine Books, Inc., 1979), p. 109.
3. Skip Ross and Carole Carlson, *Say Yes to Your Potential* (Waco, Texas: Word Books, 1983), p. 146.
4. Norman Vincent Peale, *The Power of Positive Thinking* (Old Tappan, New Jersey: Fleming H. Revell Company, 1966), pp. 110, 111.
5. W. Clement Stone, *The Success System That Never Fails* (Englewood Cliffs, New Jersey: Prentice-Hall, Inc., 1962), p. 141.
6. Joe Girard and Stanley H. Brown, *How to Sell Anything to Anybody* (New York: Warner Books, Inc., 1979), p. 129.
7. Dr. Neil Warren, *Make Anger Your Ally* (New York: Doubleday and Co., Inc., 1983), p. 16.
8. Stone, *Success System*, p. 58.

Chapter 11
The Power of Saying Thanks

1. Dale Carnegie, *How to Win Friends and Influence People* (New York: Pocket Books, 1982), p. 30.
2. Tom Hopkins, *How to Master the Art of Selling* (New York: Warner Books, Inc., 1984), pp. 245, 246.
3. W. Clement Stone, *The Success System That Never Fails* (New York: Pocket Books, 1983), p. 166.
4. Robert H. Schuller, *Tough Times Never Last, But Tough People Do!* (New York: Bantam Books, 1984), pp. 23, 24.